CONSCIOUSNESS

By Janine Canan

POETRY

Mystic Bliss

Ardor: Poems of Life

In the Palace of Creation: Selected Works 1969—1999

Changing Woman

Love, Enter

Goddess Poems

Her Magnificent Body: New & Selected Poems

Shapes of Self

Who Buried the Breast of Dreams

Daughter

Of Your Seed

STORIES

Journeys with Justine

Walk Now in Beauty: The Legend of Changing Woman

ESSAYS

My Millennium: Culture, Spirituality and the Divine Feminine

Goddesses, Goddesses: Essays by Janine Canan

TRANSLATIONS

Under the Azure: Poems of Francis Jammes

Star in My Forehead: Selected Poems by Else Lasker-Schüler

ANTHOLOGIES

Love Is My Religion, volumes 1, 2, & 3, by Mata Amritanandamayi

Garland of Love: 108 Meditations by Mata Amritanandamayi

Messages from Amma: In the Language of the Heart

She Rises like the Sun: Invocations of the Goddess by Contemporary American Women Poets

CONSCIOUSNESS

poems

JANINE CANAN

Breezeway Books

2020

ISBN: 978-1-62550-6047
Library of Congress Number
Manufactured in the United States of America.
First Edition, 2020

OM CINMAYAI NAMAH

To MATA AMRITANANDAMAYI—
Mother, Supreme Teacher and Love Itself.
With gratitude to my parents and grandmother
Mary, Lewis and Flora Burford,
many guides along the way,
sisters everywhere
and the great soul J S Bach

DEAR READER

Viewing the evening sky —
squiggly clouds, light blue —
I ask myself, What am I doing here?
I don't mean anything small like what am I doing
in this room, this town, this country.
What am I doing here on this planet now?
I know there is a reason and have spent my life
trying to find out exactly what it is.

Some things seem clear, certain duties
or dharmas, as they say in the East.
But surely I did not come here just to write
two or three inspiring poems
and put bandages on a thousand or so sufferers.
You and I, Reader, are the kind that seek enlightenment.
We want more but are not always evolved enough
to achieve more than glimmers.

Isn't it frustrating? Not that I am not grateful
for the visions I have had — you may know a few,
thanks to my guru Murdoch, who long ago gently
commanded me.
Time runs out for this incarnation — so much I treasured
in this world
is already gone and this vessel body is crumbling.
To the supreme Being — to the outermost limits — I cry:
"Take me now to the fiery heart of absolute Truth.
I feel ready, and if I am not — make me!"

TABLE OF
CONTENTS

CONSCIOUSNESS

MIND

A few bits of knowledge
floating in a vast sea
of Mystery.

FIRST WORD

African Mother spoke the first word.
Was it *ah?*
It fell on dark ears
like raindrops on thirsting soil.
Seedlings sprang up offering green to the Sun
and to humanity golden fruit
sweet and bitter.

HOMELESS

A homeless man named Death
squats on my nose
like a captain surveying the ocean.

How many others see him
I do not know, but it doesn't really matter —
he is ideal for my voyage.

Leaves bulge with stunning light.
Life surges and pours out sweet nectar.
By now he has access to all my precious treasure.

When my body goes, he will need a new perch —
but I would prefer it if we simply merged
together into the Eternal.

GOLDEN GODDESS

All the mantras
that can ever be chanted
shower gold-dust on your feet.
When You walk, the whole universe
lights up with brilliant suns.

Golden Goddess, whose only form
is Love's illumination,

Mother of Creation, Vibration of Bliss,
who can ever know or not know You—
the Self of all that is.

EXTREME

Amma, You are so extreme!
But then, You are Infinity.
And what do I who crawl like a snail
know of the extremes?
Can't You skip me ahead to some
idyllic stretch of what makes You so beautiful,
loving, overflowing and transforming,
sweet, playful, pure and free.

INCOMPREHENSIBLE

And yet so . . . beautiful.

WEB

An endless web
stretches from the mind
to the Infinite.
Everything is caught
in its vibrating threads—
embedded in the sublime design
of the Supreme Designer.

PRIESTESS SAPPHO

Aphrodite's daughter,
priestess Sappho,
singer with lyre—
into whose ear whispered
lovely Erato and holy Polymnia—
touching the foot of the Great Goddess
turned into gold.
In Alexandria's relentless blaze
her song rises immortal.

THE SEER

A poet does not write
to find out what she thinks
but to open to the great Song
and hear what it thinks.

SUNLIGHT

Appreciation is not much of a word —
it could have been made to sound sweeter.
But whether faint, warm-hearted, enthusiastic,
thundering or silent — held deep inside in secret —
it brightens like the sun
and nothing more is needed.

SORROW

Are they ever sad in heaven?
Do the angels ever weep?
Do soft clouds burst with sympathy?
Do the enlightened sometimes grieve?
Do souls on vacation gaze down, remembering?
Does the Great Mind look up from her timeless play

and allow a tear to roll down her cheek
from her all-seeing Eye?

WHAT IS ART?

Art is creation,
communication,
communion,
the body divine,
the blessed sacrament.

THE SECRET SMILE

As a child I wanted to leave this ignorant land.
But I was born here for some reason.
This may be a dream but something
is totally real: what you and I truly are,
what makes Creation and is eternal.
No matter how painful, it is bliss.

How can this be? asks the doubting mind
ceaselessly trying to figure it out.
Answers bubble and fade.
Our real home is the Source of beauty,

possibility and love pure as the purest stream.
The Soul smiles, You are all me.

BEAM

A shaft
of You:
Joy.

KANSAS CLOUDS

As I stepped quietly down the stairs
into the large sunny kitchen,
Aunt Margaret smiled
wiping her hands on her white apron.
All the pies had already been baked
and all the cows milked.
I opened the back door into rows of tall corn
waving in the warm wind.
A stocky red horse pulled the iron plow.
Clouds came tumbling down the sky
and I went out to meet them.

— *To the Burfords and the Coxes*

SAINT

A sweet Saint sat upon nothingness.
Slowly my reactions subsided into silence
and the music of our celestial conversation
faded into the Eternal.

WOMAN, A CIRCLE

At first she is not a woman
but a baby innocent and free,
who will soon become a girl balancing,
appealing, skilled and fine.

At twenty, too beautiful for words,
pure energy not quite directed;
at thirty she is more sober,
grounded, rounded and real.

In her forties she is most glorious.
Petals gush in primal splendor —
power, beauty and intelligence
all one.

In her fifties, a woman rarely gushes
but down deep a wide steady stream
knows where it is going
and cannot be stopped.

In her sixties signs of decay —
wrinkled, stained, stiffly drooping.
Older but wiser she makes fewer mistakes —
there is no time.

Seventy, pressing her face to the window
she can see the other side
and is busy preparing
and tidying.

Eighties — so much lost now —
she simply smiles and fades,
one day at a time, back to the Earth
from which she came — to the Source of it all.

— To Kimberly Moore

SNOOZING IN HEAVEN

A thousand blessings were pouring on me
and I didn't notice.
A thousand brilliant boons
but I was dozing.
Then She flashed her dazing white light
and I woke up!

RESURRECTION

A thousand miles on my belly
in the dust, prostrating to Thee.
Walking through fire, stripped
inside and out, purging mind and body.
Resurrection so arduous,
it must not be reimagined or relived.
Time, I stepped over you like a boulder—
now where do I go?

HERE

Attention, please!
Come to the present.
Here—wherever you gaze—
even with your eyes closed—
I will fill you
with sparkling joy!

*Divine Mother is the only
guru. — Swami Rama*

TALES OF A YOGI

A young man steps out of a cave into the first light,
as dark clouds roll in from Bengali bay.
With staff and notebook, he climbs
through forests of rhododendron, orchid and lily
followed by a large black bear.
"Hail to the Mother!"
he chants on his way to the peaks.

✻

"You are meant to be adored—
too beautiful to be here all alone!"
Shaking her head among the snowy rocks
the Blue Lotus replied: "Do you think I am lonely
here, one with everything?
If you pluck me, my fragrance will spread
and my purpose will be fulfilled."

✻

Meditating under the banyan tree
the old yogi asks the youth why he has come.
"For a mantra," he answers.
"Then you must wait." Days later the yogi says,
"I have a mantra but you must promise
to remember it wherever you are—in prison, even hell.
Always be happy."
"Too late!" says the River Sage as he drops his body.

Day and night his disciples fight over it.
Suddenly it bolts up, "Get out, you
foolish Hindus, Christians and Muslims —
I belong only to God! Son,
be yourself, be yourself, he repeats,
disappearing into the river.

❋

Rama slips on some pine needles,
rolls over the cliff and is speared by a branch.
He calls out to the gods, but there is no reply.
"The body is mortal but I am eternal," he reminds
himself.
Above, a woman shouts, "A dead man!" He waves his
limbs
and she pulls him up. His Master appears: "Today
was the day of your death — but I gave you some of my
years."

❋

"If you will not show me God, I will leave," Rama
sulks.
'Tomorrow," his Master replies.
All night Rama prays for God to reveal himself.
At sunrise the master asks, "What kind of God
do you wish to see? If I show you the truth,
you will not believe it.
First you need to know your Self."

"I am going to drown myself! I have sacrificed
everything and now I cannot even enjoy life."
"Suicide won't solve your problems —
in your next life you will face them again.
But if you insist, tie on rocks or you will start
swimming."
As Rama ties on the rocks, his Master touches his
brow
dissolving his thoughts, and Rama drowns in an ocean
of Bliss.

EQUILIBRIUM

Balance of masculine and feminine is the goal —
but how can we know what balance is?
When we have dragged one wing
for thousands of years,
how can we know how to fly?
For ages, women have been hiding
to avoid rape, battery, stoning, hanging and burning.
Gradually, they are emerging — crushed
and yet beautiful, broken-hearted and yet caring still —
inconceivably beautiful women.
This is not a war so much as an upheaval —
a vast uprising of women onto the face of the earth —
confusing men who thought they were in control

and are beginning to realize they were never
the power that moves all things.
Women tried manning up to be considered equal.
But men have to posture down, deflate
their gross egos, refine their violent behavior
and play a supportive role
in saving our devastated world.

It is not men's fault that they were raised
to believe they were born to dominate.
But that belief is wrong!
And has caused inconceivable suffering.
Give it up, men, return to reality.

Kneel before a bird, a bee, a cloud,
a mountain, wave or woman
and listen to her point of view.
Earth has heard your opinions for millennia —
it does not need to hear them anymore.

HUMAN

Becoming a human being
is like carving a beautiful sculpture.
Every morning I wake, step before the stone
and resume the endless work.

EONS

Bees and elephants,
are you going away?
Human beings, are you going too?
Earth, have you had enough of us?
Must we mutate into something better?
Will the oceans cover you with crystalline blue
and the Sun blaze forth its eonic glory?
And Now, as always, bulge effulgent
with unsayable Love.

MOTHER NATURE

Be like Nature.
If you keep opposing Her,
what good will that do?
Irresistible and indestructible,
She is our foundation, our resource,
our very ground.

MERCY

Beloved Mother Earth,
may You one day rest again in peace,
no longer violently and heartlessly abused
by your own children.
Have mercy on us!

SHOW ME

Beloved, why are You not here?
I know you are here but where are you?
I know You are hiding in the silence,
vibrating in the emptiness,
shining in the invisible.
Show me where!
Do not make me wait any longer —
oh Beloved, show me where.

TRIPLE GODDESS

Bountiful Lakshmi,
nourish, heal and beautify us.
Awesome, fearsome Kali,
humble, purify and change us.
Sublime Saraswati, teach and sing us
to the highest being.

Triple Goddess of a thousand names and powers,
shower your divine blessings upon us forever.

CHALLENGES

Bridges are everywhere —
may we cross them.
Karmas are passing —
may we altar or accept them.
Everything is worthy —
may we find what is precious and true.

ALL LIT UP

Brilliant suns everywhere!
All my centers on fire.
I am a bustling city
that never turns off its lights.
Goddess, You outdo yourself
cranking up the current—
I am electric!

FEAST

Cautiously, we sample the appetizers.
Suddenly, at the end of the banquet
as the waiters are clearing away the dishes,
we develop a voracious appetite!

Why wait until the meal is over?
Why not help ourselves
to all the exquisite delights
spread before us now.

SACRED

Choose a sacred name
and become it — otherwise,
why disturb the silence?

All this information — what is it for?
Knowledge is inside us —
may we discover it!

Only inner work really works.
The world will never be joyful until we are —
stop grinding your axe.

In a moment we will be gone.
Is this really how we long
to spend our lives?

FRIENDSHIP

Competition is the vampire
who sucks blood from a bond
and grimaces when you win.

Compassion is the angel
who rubs balm on any wound
and sings at every success.

BEYOND

Creation is made
of darkness and light.
Demons wrestle with gods
in mysteries beyond our understanding.

CREATIVITY

Creativity is the last step
before God.

No, it is God Itself.

MELTDOWN

Crowned by the eons
You stand, golden Goddess,
holding in your hands the molten mass
of my soul—placed there
when this body began its fireworks
of mortality.

Through You I have life, breath,
happiness and love.

All these are immortal and never cease.
In the wind blows the dust of millions of years —
dreamy forms enticing and empty.
But You, Great Mother, are boundlessly beyond.

Unharmed in the blaze,
I gaze at You in pure trust
and You stroke me tenderly.
We continue our play so deep
only the Supreme knows.
And gradually Love melts me down.

LIGHTS!

Culture is a vastly beautiful woman.
Why dress her like a whore
cowering in the dark.
Turn on the lights,
please!

THE CROWN

Daylight saving-time—
fake jewel in the cardboard crown
of the fool who hallucinates
he controls Nature.

Take off your boorish crown!
Let the Sun show you daylight
and darkness that is real.
Let the Moon reveal her colossal tides.

And Divinity tell her clock-less time.
Listen to the Earth — her martyred trees,
her howling children, her unyielding women.
Save yourselves!

Open your tiny hearts and discover
the eternal Source,
the true power of humility,
innocence, compassion and remorse.

Surrender! — for transformation
is inescapable.

INVITATION TO A WEDDING

Dear Friends, my darling and I request
the pleasure of your company.
Expect no bride in white for purity —
who can claim that in this age of promiscuity?
No vows of fidelity — couples who sacrifice
and forgive may last, but we are no liars.

Marriage serves man's power and comfort only.
So suppress your laughter
when we gush our adorations.
At least our bond to our mothers will last.
And hold your tongue about the reasons
none should be joined in patrimony.

We panic at the thought of our own company,
so as long as men rule the world
please join in our doomed game of happiness.
One day life will be different
and love will come naturally.
In the end, it is all there is.

MESSAGE

Master, your message
is impressed in every cell —
even my blood murmurs it.
It whispers in the moon
sings from the stars,
wakes the sleeping,
heals the hurt
and strengthens the limping.
Thank you, precious Sage
for your eternal guiding Light.

VEIL

Death
is only a thin veil
hanging between us
and eternity.

WELLSPRING

Descend through your own depths
to where the water springs forth
and flows eternally.

SANCTUM

Divine Body, gift of the Goddess,
every cell luminous with love and magic —
patient, wise and laughing.
Through you passes all knowing,
softly kissing each atom like a child.
Glory dwells in all things.
There is nothing in this world
that is not suffused with divine Light,
wisdom, beauty and delight.

BEYOND PRAISE!

Divine Mother is beyond.
Out there — in here — down there —
beyond, beyond, beyond!
Praise!

Divine Mother is the supreme Miracle
whose only action is the making of miracles.
For She invented the miraculous
and is the mind behind every miracle,
the great lover of miracles.
All miracles reflect Her
and rejoice in her delight!

Praise Her, praise
and praise Her!

WELCOME

Does Mother say, "Murderer, molester—go away!
You are greedy, angry, heartless, shallow,
judgmental, self-centered—go away!"
No, even to a demon she says, "Stay near
where you will cause less harm.
Come to Mother and let her try to open your heart
and keep you from falling to the very bottom of the
abyss.
I am with you no matter how unaware you are,
how misled, how low you have fallen."
She does not say, "I am too high
to speak to you or touch you."
To the supreme height of Consciousness
She welcomes all.

LOVE

Do what you love to do.
Love what you do.

Let everything you do
be Love for Love
from Love.

It's all Love.

SUPREME

Dragonflies and seekers of truth,
even the rocks worship You.
You are the Universe.
You are Consciousness.
You are All.

VAST TRAP

Drawn irresistibly into your web
I was caught in a vast trap of Love
where You are me
and I am You
and the majesty of Love
spreads to infinity.

OPEN

Every religion in the Palace of Humanity
has a beautiful window
that opens to God.

New windows keep on being added
until everyone emerges
into the Open.

NARCISSUS

Ego basks in his sunny ignorance,
afloat in his vapid stupor,
endlessly circling the shallows . . . of Self.

TRANSFORMATIONS

Even the dead are beautiful
in your presence.
In the stream of your beauty
they rise and reform.
Oh Goddess,
You are the starlight in winter,

the full moon rising,
the returning Sun,
the dance of fire,
the power of oceans,
the fragrance of flowers,
the magic of poetry.
In the alchemy of your Love
everything is transformed.
Even the dead smile again,
oh Goddess.

ON THE ROAD

Ever been tapped on the shoulder by a Muse
and dragged by your hair to pen and paper?
That's Inspiration! Why not leave those other jottings
to the trash bin of the mind?
Workshops, classes—maybe it's best to simply read.
There are so many books already
that nobody wants to read—wouldn't it be better
to serve hot soup to somebody hungry?

Inspiration—what is it anyway?
Where does it come from? Some Goddess
you haven't met yet? Why not get out on the road
and keep walking until you meet Her!

AVATARA

Every inch of her body
is pure *darshan* —revelation —
a showing —an opening —
streaming, numinous
and holy.

BLESSINGS

Every moment is a blessing —
an opportunity to be Love,
to forget our illusions
and melt into infinite
Consciousness.

OMNISCIENT

Everything
has one of your Eyes
gazing
everywhere.

PARADOX

Everything I said was the voice
of someone who knew nothing
and yet was the voice
of everything.

MIRACLE

Everything is a miracle
and once in a while
it becomes obvious
even to our minds.

PARTICIPATION

When in doubt,
assume it is a miracle.
When a miracle is being performed
on our behalf, shouldn't we
enthusiastically
join in?

RED FLAGS

Everything is a sign.
Every leaf
is a prayer for life.

DIVINE CONSCIOUSNESS

Everything is full of God.
Genius is pure humility.

Few seek Self-knowledge —
what treasure they are!

Wisdom is the bliss
of the Cosmos.

Deeper drafts of grief
require greater illumination.

Here, take this drink
of intoxicating Joy!

THE BOOK

Everything is your Book!
I turn its spellbinding pages
one after the other
and cannot stop.
Why would I want
to read any other?
Author, jail me
in your infinite joy.

OR

Everything
that human beings have learned,
step by step,
over tens of thousands of years
is ours now —
to be passed on
or —

LET US STOP

Every time I accept a plastic bag
I feel a pain near my heart,
knowing its fumes will poison the air
and one day it will strangle a fish.
Oh Humanity, can't we stop
causing all this pain?

THE SPLENDOR

Every uncanny part of Her
bulges effulgent
with God!
Manna, prana,
lumen and numen —
sweet blazing Sun of Love!

SPEECH

Every word could be a word
for God, don't you think?
Every word
God.

THIS OR THAT

Every word is an infinite understatement.
No wonder so many sages
refer to reality as simply *This* or *That*.
Or remain silent —
or burst in glee.

FLAMENCAS

Flamencas, your whirling red skirts drip blood
as empires come conquering — taking you
for entertainment, raping you for thrills.
Black heels drill the tarred Earth
and old Crones shriek, *Olé!*

Golden-haired, jet and ochre,
your arms ripple skyward, your dresses shower stars,
your smiles a chorus of Light!
Entranced in creation your lay it on —
sisters of Bliss, lead us on, *Olé!*

And Mother's darling Shakti boys,
good of the Earth, wanderers unforgotten,
all you children of throbbing hearts —
learn every lesson you need
to live in joy and flame *Olé!*

Grandmothers weep who nursed
from wombs, tits, embracing arms. No one
can ever take your power away—though men flexing
muscles ooze their grief from battle to battle,
seed the world with despair and remorse—sapping,
souring, destroying, *Nolé!*

Never fail to nourish, to inspire, to be!
No one can steal your secret, no way! Fire the world
with the force you draw from your own true Self—
womb, egg, mitochondria—concentrate, purify,
beautify, increase and pass Life on—
Love flames, Flamencas, *Olé, Olé, Olé!*

—Barcelona 2003

PROPHECY

For over five thousand years
mothers have slaved and had no say,
owning nothing, not even their bodies,
brutalized at any man's whim,
routinely tortured and, slaughtered—only a few
at extreme cost gaining partial freedom.

Today the mothers wake amid the disaster
and bond with a roar! As the men pump

themselves up with *more* testosterone,
weapons, vulgarity, sex, cruelty,
lies and greed—unwilling to surrender
one speck of their pitiless power.

They will do anything to grab and gobble
more, wallowing in their rotten might.
Ruder, cruder and more violent—grotesques
of sadistic pride—they finish
goodness and righteousness altogether,
crushing the last of their very own lineages.

Oceans rise, mountains sink, plants shrivel up,
bones and plastic coat the earth.
Her molten core sloshes wildly
shifting poles and melting glaciers.
Forests became swamps and farmlands deserts.
Streams of refugees parade to their death
and cities drown in the sea.

History, morality, culture, language,
knowledge have become relics, as sickly man fades
away. Will some survive—in Finland? Ireland?
Grecian caves? Bihar? Kauai? South Africa?
Will Hopi still grow corn?
Life's natural beauty and harmony will remain.
Diamonds will fill the nighttime skies.
The spiral of Creation, turning on its luminous axis,
will resume its majestic play.

BOASTFUL CHILDREN

For the ultimate Victory
children need parents not coaches.
Need love that is selfless
and values that do not change.
Awareness of others, not only themselves.
Need to be taught to be humble saints
not ostentatious celebrities.

GOD'S EYE

Georgia OK was sent
to make paintings for God.
White pelvis
on Changing Woman's mountain.

Black cross
on raspberry clouds.
A pool of pure blue sky.
Pink tile steps, velvety jimson curtains,
dark rooms into the open.

Eyes thinning until there was nothing
between her and Infinity.
A whole universe
in a white Rose.

A pink petunia,
God's Eye.

REVELATION

Glorious as the Sun —
reveal your Self!

IN YOU

God became you.
Take refuge in your God-self.
Everything —
pure Consciousness —
is within you.

PRAYER

Goddess, all I have to offer
is my ego — everything else is Yours.
With every fiber I long to rid myself

of this pitiful, paltry, burdensome delusion.
And yet I cannot do even that—it sticks like glue.
No matter how hard I twist and tug it will not budge.

You are a Goddess, in fact *the* Goddess—
can't you think of something that won't kill me, to
remove it?
Your imagination is infinite.
You are the most creative Force that exists.
You created this world and all the invisible universes.
There is no end to your creations.

This petty dark thing
with its inane opinions, irritations and naive ideas
doesn't belong here, isn't really part of me—ugly,
annoying, it plagues me like a blood-sucking mosquito.
Mother, helplessly I offer it from my heart's depths
to your supreme domain.

No matter how long I have to live with it,
I will always know it is not real or right and cannot be
trusted.
It is a speck in my eye to return with this passing body
to the earth.
You who know everything, who have proven to me
that You are Love Itself,
please help me solve this problem.

OH

Goddess Saraswati grabbed me
and will not let me go!
We are plunging over the cascades,
crashing onto the roiling river,
charging onward toward some Ocean, they say,
but I have never seen, oh Shyama,
what am I, your seeming child, supposed to hold onto?
This pure Energy, this overwhelming Power,
this supreme Force has swept me totally out of control
and Yes! I say it, I pronounce it, I am helpless
in this unnamable and forever unnamed.

Oh Vak, I give up! Divinest Beauty,
sacred-most Knowledge, treasure of Language,
subtlest music of Creation — these pitiful words
will never crawl anywhere near
the nearest edge of what you Are.
And I who have always been your adoring slave
am now nothing more than yours.
Oh annihilating One!!!
Oh Goddess!

                    — to Laura Ambika Gati Amazzone

CHILD

God is a child, You say.
A play queen
who lives in everything.
I love her most when she
delights in me.

CRACKED

God is a seed
cracked open
blazing!

FIRST ENCOUNTER

"Oh get her blessing!"
the women chorused
and lifted me onto her lap
where nothing but measureless Shakti vibrated —
Creation's pure essence — timeless placeless
bodiless, mindless —
I was gone — there was nothing
but That.

SACRED

Great books are stars
descended from heaven
to share their inmost secrets.
How can we hold their blazing pages
in our trembling hands?
If not for the dark letters covering their pages,
their light would blind us.

MEMORIAM

Half-men, half-machine, some women
hardly qualify as women.
Lost is their feminine grace,
motherly way, creative power
and boundless care, their exquisite refinement,
immortal wisdom, sweet modesty,
deep humility, boundless patience —
their ability to listen, their terrifying ferocity
and devastating honesty — their monumental courage,
commitment and endless sacrifice.

Who these are, nobody knows.
So many gone — I grieve the disappeared
who pretend to be women.
I mourn the missing.

I want to call them home
but they do not want to be called.
I cry out to our Mother.
My tears wet their empty coffins and urns.
Their ashes scatter in the winds.

EVOLUTION

Have we reached the peak of immorality?
Have we hit rock-bottom?
When will we cycle out of the Iron Age—
the dark age, the age of materialism,
the hardest and yet most auspicious age
for enlightenment?

Have mercy, Healer,
fix us with your subtle surgery
and cure this plague of selfishness.
And if that cannot be done, grant us the peace
and patience of the eternal.

FOREVER

Her divine countenance
pervades the cosmos,
every cell primordially alive,
unfathomable, irresistibly magnetic.
We are inseparable
and locked together forever.

FATE

Here She comes
in her mad unstopping overflow
into and through us—more God than ever,
more God and more!

HALFWAY

Here we are—babes of Consciousness—
one foot in, one foot out,
afloat in the cosmos,
buried in the sand.

REALIZATION

Here we sit in our wall-less prison.
Once we realize this,
we will be enlightened.

WAVES

Her last phrase was swallowed up
in endless waves
of Silence.

OPEN

Honestly, I have chosen very little.
I open myself and am told—who tells me?
I feel joy and I dance,
every cell overflowing ecstatically.
And I know this is right.
I open and her Presence is there and never leaves.
There is nothing to choose
because it is all One.

LIFE

Hopefully
we grow as we go.

AMONG THE MOTHERY MOSUO

"How do you choose your matriarch?"
inquired the anthropologist.
"So easy!" the sisters laughed,
"she was always the most caring!"

"How many children do you have
with three sisters — three?"
"Oh no! — one or two — we have
so many other things to do!"

The men playing pool she asked, laughing,
"Are you lazy — you don't seem to work
as much as the women." "— We fish, herd the animals,
build houses, run messages to the clans.

The women plant, harvest, preserve,
cook food; sew and tell the stories —
they take care of everyone!
They do more work."

"What if you fall in love?" she asked.

"We lay flowers at the door
and if our love is returned, it opens.
In the morning we return to our clan."

"What if you wish to marry?"
"No problem." "If you want to divorce?"
 "No problem — marriage is purely
a matter of the heart."

—from *Im Matriarchat der Mosuo*,
documentary by Heide Goøttner-
Abendroth

DARK CENTURIES

How many urns of ash have been poured
on your feet, great Banyan?
How many incinerated women
have nurtured your massive roots
and long imploring arms?

How many beautiful toiling women
have been wasted
by men's measureless contempt
for his creator, mother and teacher?

How many innocent lives
will fertilize your weeping branches,

oh mocked Tree, for how many more
painful dark centuries?

GOD THE ROCK

How She must love everything
She has created.
I saw Her hard as a rock,
cosmic, black, imploded, condensed to nothing —
all her radiance withdrawn —
inscrutable Consciousness reveling
in a limitless hole where powerful, humming, light-
swallowing Energy
sucked everything to the center
of her boundlessly fecundating heart.
How She must love everything
She became, has become and is becoming
as She showers and terminates her earth-shaking
displays
to the ends of the blazing universe —
eternally and blissfully becoming and unbecoming —
forever God.

— To Sarala McClain

GARDENER

All day and night
you nurture us, watering our soil,
quenching our roots,
rising up our stems
to make us leafy and green.
Every bud you nourish
with the glorious sunbeams
of your smile and eventually
our petals loosen.
Oh Gardener, you are so patient
and we are so slow.
We offer our hearts
because we know that you love us.
Help us to open all the way
and make your garden divinely beautiful.
May all your blossoms be kissed
with sparkling dew.

THE CALL

I always felt Death near.
Now it rubs against me like a temple cat.
How does it feel? Not bad,
but I cannot say there is no anxiety.
Will I have time to finish Mother's projects?

And that brings up the question again:
What is my assignment?

At thirteen I heard the call to healing and poetry.
Mentors, guides, sages met me
along the way—in books and music,
on the streets, in trees and clouds and ocean waves.
Plans appeared as if on the pages
of a divine Book written
by the Great Queen.

Joyfully I journeyed, in love with life,
every leaf—yet detached as a star
burning beyond dualities,
dream worlds, bones, dust.
Mother was always singing,
"Spread your petals, my flower,
offer your fragrance everywhere."

CYCLE OF CIVILIZATIONS

I always felt like a shoot on a branch of a long
tradition—
a legacy continuing from the Paleolithic and before,
that rose from Mother Africa hundreds of thousands of
years ago,
peopling the Earth in waves spreading over Arabia,

round India to Indonesia and aboriginal Australia;
then twenty thousand years later,
a family migrating north to the Caucasus
where several thousand years later they forked —
East, crossing the Bering Strait to Turtle Island, south
to Tierra del Fuego,
and West all over Europe — always leaving their life-
prints,
thoughts and visions inscribed and painted on rock,
leaf, ice and wood, then printed on paper,
bound in books, read on computers.

But today it seems that all these — computer, book,
tree —
may soon strew vast deserts as mountains
crumble into finer and finer dust
in the harsh blast of the Sun
and clutter the colossal seas that engulf most of the
planet.
Who then among the remaining
will remember the thousands of languages
painstakingly created and preserved by human beings
for eons?
Who will even know how to recognize the wild edibles,
unsalty waters and grassy grains?

Will survivors gather round a fire under the brilliant
sky
to tell the stories they barely recall?
Will they sing and dance and pray to Mother Moon

and the stars, waking before dawn to go hunting
for water, berries, nuts, roots, mushrooms and
greens —
marking rocks and caves with their signs as they pass?
This has happened before.
Will the cascading stream of human culture —
story, song, medicine, science and sacred texts —
that today flows from books,
run dry and narrow as the mighty Saraswati
that today yields only a few drops?

THE SMILE

I always see the beatific smile
of Ramana Maharsi, cross-legged
in loincloth in his brick niche,
radiating from the page of a book.

White-haired, slender, his belly
an open wound of maggots feasting on cancer,
totally removed from human pain
and the limits of the physical body.

One day when I was searching for the book
in vain, I was shocked to learn
that the great saint's final disease was not
in the belly —like mine—but in his arm.

Ramana's arm was tended, bandaged and clean.
Could it have been another yogi
whose picture I had seen? But so vividly
I remembered his wound and smiling face.

Pure light suffused the photograph
of the fully illuminated Master,
seated in lotus posture in his meditation cave,
dying in bliss.

After some time I understood.
Long before my own illness—untouched by time or
space—
a great soul had graciously shown me how to smile like
the Sun
even when Death is devouring your body.

How to smile in bliss no matter what!
And now, pure Divine Being would like me
to share my incandescent photo
with you.

AQUAMARINE

I am a word,
nothing but a word
swimming among words

in beautiful vortices,
crystalline blue waters
where I have been swimming
for eternities.

LETTING GO

I am dropping words
one by one
into the River —

golden coins
shimmering
in the Incalculable.

THE PROMISE

"I am perfect," says Perfection
as I fret over my imperfections.
"What imperfections?" She asks, "I don't see any."
 "These deadheads have to be plucked
before I can blossom fully."

"Perfect!" She smiles.
"At the perfect time
I will gladly do it for you."

YOUR GRACE

I ask only one small thing —
to merge in You.

ALL DIVINE

I bow to You, Most Glorious,
in your forms of Knowledge
and of Ignorance —
to You I humbly bow.

INITIATION

I came on my knees
and drowned in the oceanic lap
of the living Goddess.
There was no time, place, direction —
only energy, connection, Love.
But I had never known
That Love before.
I was undone — gone
in her infinite power —
oned with All
that Is.

UNTITLED

I cannot remember anything
before this moment.
Can You?

MEMORY

I do not remember our audience
with Pope Pius XII in Rome.
I remember so little of even this life.
The small brain keeps little—lets some things
flow through, takes a few notes,
tosses them into the corner,
later into the trash.

When we die, brain too is tossed—
buried in earth or burned to ash
in a blazing bonfire.
Memory is mere poetry—
an artful arrangement of pictures,
words afloat in the nowhere
somewhere.

CONSCIOUS

I exhale three Oms,
step to the marble bowl,
rinse my face
in pure watery consciousness
and the bowl twinkles.

I dry myself
in the conscious green towel,
lift the sponge and wipe
the vibrating sink.
"I like it this way," smiles the sink.

Then I write it on papery waves
of consciousness.
How do I do this, I marvel,
when I am nothing
but streaming consciousness?

POETRY

I have turned into poetry.
Every cell of my body is a poem.
Every molecule is a word.
Every atom a letter.
What magic this body
that hums this song.

SPARKS

If I were a fully realized human being
aware of the divinity —
absolute Consciousness —
in everyone; if I could see God
in every selfish human being.
In the trees, the stones, the waves —
oh, that is easy — but if I could see divinity
in every pair of agonizing eyes,
goodness haloing godly bodies,
talents radiating to the Cosmic Sea.

If I could see past lives and future,
and know which the next step we need to take.
See that every cell is made of nothing
but Love's generosity.
And always know that I am made
of God's supreme Beauty — oh then,
having reached that final goal,
touching that Truth, all would sparkle
in perfection and happiness,
and my light spark your light too.

SWAN SONG

If I were a swan,
I would not say a word.
I would glide on the silken surface
sending ripples of beauty
to the very edge.
Glide in my silence
and dive and disappear.

ENTRANCE

If Jesus opens your heart,
worship Him.
If a tree speaks to your heart,
worship It.

The doors are endless —
open and enter.

THE DREAM

If only man loved life
the way he loves machines,
respected Creation
the way he respects information,
worshipped beauty the way he worships money,
adored the Earth the way he adores power.

If only man craved kindness
the way he craves sex,
enjoyed reducing suffering the way he enjoys causing it.
Would listen instead of know it all.
Became more humane
instead of more hideous.

If only man had not gone astray
a very long time ago.
Would leave the world alone
for one day
of peace.

ABCS

If we do not honor the plants
and animals and stones,
we will drop dead —
it is that simple.

SUNLIGHT

If we do not open the curtains wide,
how will the Sun shine in
and illuminate
this darkening age?

IN SPIRIT

If you find this poem
in some time remote to me,
know that I am with you
in the Spirit that never dies.

If you discover these lines
somewhere I have never been
and they wake in your heart —
know that I am with you as the Love in all things.

If you feel my breath some place
far from me but near to you,
you will know me
in the Truth that erases time.

If you find these words and understand,
know that we are One —
the undivided Splendor
that unites all things.

CHILDREN

If you live in idiotic times —
try to laugh
not cry.

PREPARATION

If you see in my eyes
a distance that goes all the way,
know that I am preparing to go the distance —
opening my eyes to more light,
my body to more good,
my heart to more love.
Mother, open me totally so that I
may be one with You.

ASKING FOR IT

I had had enough and cried to Mother,
"I don't want to die like this —
it's not good enough! I know
I don't deserve it but could You please,
out of your infinite compassion,

just take me up one rung on the ladder?"

The next morning in every room,
wherever I went, I could feel
the subtle energy radiating.
This was lovely, so much better,
and I was happy, so happy
that after a month I became greedy
and thoughtlessly cried out,

"Oh Mother, this is so wonderful.
"If one rung is this much greater,
could You please take me up a bunch of rungs!"
And I meant it.
Soon after, diagnosed with a fatal illness,
I was taken to the next level.

AT THE OCEAN

I have arrived at the inner Ocean
great and gleaming.
It is calling me in.
I descend
into her boundless embrace,
tumbling in the turbulent tides,
sinking deeper and deeper
into her heart

all the way to the clear point
of absolute Light —
dissolved at last.

THE CRY

I heard You singing across the Cosmos
to Kali, the Great One,
your voice — can it even be called
a *voice*? — rising, scorching,
incinerating the night.

All the agony of human experience
You poured out in supplication!
What were You pleading for,
crying for, demanding
on our behalf?

Some grace to save us from sinking
under the rim of Creation forever?
Only You knew.
From the heart of Divinity rose
that searing sound.

For You know no separation
from Her.
And yet that agony,

that excruciating caring
for us here.

— *To Mata Amritanandamayi,
Ammritapuri, India*

JOY

I just go from joy to joy.
How can this be *?*
So pure —
this.

THE ROSE

I lie down at the foot
of the holy Rose.
I am pierced by a myriad rays
of cosmic Light.
Dross vanishes and I melt
in her infinite Grace.

DEATH

Death perches on the arch of my nose
like an old pair of spectacles
as I contemplate the landscape.

We are ancient friends.
I could never begin to tell you
about all our encounters.

As a child I recognized him
walking beside me
with his little black box of time.

Today, empty-handed,
he swings like a monkey
along the fence.

BLISS

I want to sleep
in the bliss of this Love.
To taste the bliss of this joy.
To murmur the bliss of this good.
To walk in the bliss of this Light.

DREAMS IN PROGRESS

Imagine—the Goddess thought us!
Out of laughing luminosities we came—
individualities with choices,
backgrounds vast as the universe.
We are her dreams-in-progress,
her ideas made tangible,
her desires embodied.
Imagine!

UNKNOWING

In ancient times, people
did not go to church or temple to be spiritual.
Every step they took was spiritual.

In our long search for our Source
all kinds of confusion
have arisen.

Now we need to be purified of all our assumptions,
expectations and judgments,
if we are ever to know the Truth.

BODY SCAN

In any case,
it shows
nothing
but
God.

SWEET NOTHINGS

In my favorite café, where people chatter
en Français and other glowy tongues,
it's hard to stay seated and finish my *café au lait,*
when I long to join the mothery women clearing tables,
youthful beauties serving *soupe, tarte et quiche*,
Pascale offering trays of *fraîcheur* under the oak,
and chase the aromas streaming from the kitchen
where baguettes keep levitating from the oven.

Spotting the sunny cottage with chalk-board,
Ouvert hand-written, I could hear the angels laughing
who designed it specially for me.
Inside, others sighed, "Twenty years I waited,"
"adorable!" and other phrases sweet and light
as Pascal's chouquettes. Now that we have found
this perfect haven—time-out from the bitter taste
of so much imperfection—how can we ever leave?

HIGHER LEARNING

Intellect is the elementary school of the mind.
Learn your lessons and graduate
to the high school of the heart,
where we can learn to be happy and good.

PROTECT US

In the Age of Wrong —
when evil is switched with good,
insults become compliments,
ignorance is knowledge
and lies become the prevailing truth —
oh Great Goddess, protect us
from perversion, corruption and obscenity.
Save us! Vaporize the dark demons
within and all around
in your annihilating Light.

ORIGIN

In the end
the meaning of all words

is the Silence
from which we were born.

INTERMINABLE WAR

In the shady woods
by the gurgling stream,
a little girl is playing with frogs
and gazes up at the fire-bombs exploding
over Dresden.
In a flower garden
a little girl with long black hair
freezes as the Atomic bomb
obliterates Hiroshima.

Radioactive winds
of mushrooming hydrogen bombs
blow over the children
of Los Angeles.
Every girl and boy
grows up in man's
interminable war
on Life.

Men destroy
what they want,
steal the wealth,

invent the weapons,
poisons and technologies
to sell for money and power.
This is the madness of Patriarchy
that rules and annihilates
the world.

THE DIVE

Down into the glowering,
boiling, sweaty boozy bar,
jammed with a feverish mob,
stepped the violin diva.

She might have stayed above,
playing sublime melodies to the hills
or to empty halls of entranced elders; or joined
the angels round the corner feeding the starving.

What was she thinking
as her Stradivarius began to crack and melt?
That from the debauched crowd
one or two souls might soar into the Light forever?

— To Anne-Sophie Mutter

MASTER

Into your revelations I am stirred—
heartbeat by heartbeat, cell by sparkling cell.
Into your words I am steeped,
marinated and cured.
How can I ever forget your teachings?
When I leave this life I will take them with me
wherever I go.
I will always be soaked
in You.

RELEASE

I open to the breathing of the plants,
the innocence of the animals,
the possibility of humanity,
the effort that each one makes.
Open to my own true Self which is Love
and release the solitary confinement of me,
allowing it to dissolve into the ocean of Consciousness.
Free of good and bad, error, delusion and sorrow,
I evaporate in the boundless sky
of infinite Light.

LOVE CONSCIOUSNESS

Is God getting bored with me?
Is that why I am fading?
Is She thinking her energy might be better spent
on another project?
Have I spent enough time here?

Where will I go next?
These transfers are not always easy —
some people hang on
till a friend finally turns off the machine.
Others cling like bacteria to a rock.

But for Her, everything is easy!
When She did-in the demons at the close
of the last Dark Age, She withdrew her goddesses
and with only a graceful flick
of her wrist, banished them all.

So say the ancient scriptures.
But what does somebody like me know —
a poet, who doesn't even know what she knows
but would love to know it All.
And the only way she knows how to do that is to
become Her.

Forgive me if the poet unintentionally
blasphemes against your beliefs.

Even a poet has some responsibility for her words.
But from my own point of view
they seem perfectly divine.

What if all of Creation is Mother's
infinite eternal Love Consciousness
and we became conscious of That?
This is what the poet Janine
is saying.

All she really wants is to merge in Her —
no questions asked.
And what does she expect
from such a merger?
Sublimity, Understanding and Bliss.

HER RETURN

I signed up for Mother's return.
"I'm coming too." I cried!
I gave what I had —
every moment of the flowing river.
There was nothing else —
only the waters pouring through me.
It was all I ever wanted —
the experience of her power
inundating every dreaming cell.

Yes, I said, I want to become conscious of You!
Through mortal eyes see your eternal beauty.
And so I volunteered to serve in her Creation —
one of her millions of handmaids of Love.

LOVE

Is it true?
Are we really Love?

Is Love our true nature?
It is certainly the only thing that works,
makes clear, brings happiness.

Mother, open our hearts to the source
of Love within us and everything that exists.
Show us that All is Love.

ALL

It is all
One.

That is all
there is
to it.

CHANNEL

It is hard to concentrate with you,
Death, leaning over my shoulder
making those faces.

I am trying to be a channel
for what comes and goes
and need to practice detachment a little longer.

So can't you come back
in a more inviting form
when you really require my attention?

PRAYER FOR SLEEPWALKERS

It is hard to know what to say about this world,
much less what is beyond it.
Unaware, darkness devours more
and more light and excretes it.

Unknown to the sleepers, light shines everywhere —
in the stars, the moon and tiny fireflies.
Even the sleepwalkers glow morosely
as dark songs lure them back to their cold beds.

Mother, awaken the sleepers!

Rock them in your electrifying arms!
Bring these corpses back to life!

THE TREASURE

It is not found in books —
they are merely maps.
It is buried deep
in Experience.

HUMANITY

It is not God who is dead
but humanity
that needs to be
resurrected.

TATTOO

It is not what is on your skin
that matters but what is under it,

flowing in your blood, informing your cells,
radiating holy light.

It is the design your life creates
with its thoughts, words and deeds —
the icon that demonstrates *I am life,*
I am me, I am part of the whole.

I breathe, I live, I love
and nothing can contain me.
I was tattooed by Mystery Itself
with a zillion points of light.

OBSTACLE

It isn't really the word *God*
that stands in the way,
blocking the Light,
but the big black cloud
of the ego.

COMMUNION

It is so lovely to talk to my Mother,

to talk and talk and talk
to my Mother
and never stop listening
to Her.
To hear her voice
is bliss.

THE DANCE OF JOY

Three in the morning —
darshan is over, but Amma
stays in her chair.
Priya hands her a songbook
and She browses, beginning to sing
a beautiful heart-rending melody.
Lifting her hands to one side, She claps,
then lowers, lifts and claps again —
outlining the ancient Yoni mudra.
We mirror her, press closer,
riding on Ramanand's powerful voice
to higher and higher realms of joy.

Mother sparkles in bliss to see us drunk
on all this beauty and happiness,
rising and falling in her dancing mudra of Love.
Our ecstasy knows no bounds!
We swing from the stars
as She dances from the hall.

OFFERING MY HEAD

It wasn't enough to chop off my head —
You had to do it over and over
and over until lightning
became bliss.

And so You make us change,
blood-dripping Queen
with your blade and skulls
and eyes ablaze with Eternity.
Keep on swinging then, if You must —
my head is yours anyway.
Here — why not take it
once and for all!

ON THE ROAD

It was the Sixties.
I was standing on the corner
hitchhiking in a short white dress.
An old car pulled up
and I scooted in.

The dark-haired driver sped to my destination
and as I bent over to thank him,
handed me his card: pale yellow

with a photo of Meher Baba
and *Don't worry, be happy.*

I saved the card and as the years flew
occasionally told the story,
in time adding "He even looked
like Baba with his long black hair
and curling moustache."

One day, after a number of other visionary
experiences,
it occurred to me that maybe
it *was* Meher himself.
He had once been in California.
But by the time I received his card
he was bald, living in silence in India,
It seems he crossed the world
to give me a lift and something to hold onto
until I found my way back to the Main Road.
The next year he dropped his body.

AWE

I worship the great Ah.
The awareness
that commands surrender,
devotion, obedience and adoration!

PURE

Language is a great boon
to humankind
created by the mind of God.
And poetry its purest expression.

SATSANG

Let's not waste our time gossiping
and complaining—let's talk
about our spiritual struggles
and cosmic Being.
Tell me anything you know
about that!
What do you know
about God?

THE WORD

Let the word *God*
be ground into the finest powder
and dispersed everywhere!

LET GO

Life is a dance!
When your partner moves on —
let go! Or you may stumble
and miss the next step.

WAKE UP

Life is a few hours.
Mostly we dream.

Wake and feel the peace,
the beauty and the boundless grace.

LIFE

Life is a moment.
Make the most of it.
Make it eternal.

OFFER IT!

Life is a shining diamond —
offer it to Love!
Let each day be a shining jewel
in your crown.

DANCE

Life is a succession
of annihilating austerities and blissful gestures,
a divine dance in the heart of Creation.

PATH OF FIRE

Life is austerity
no matter what luxury,
suffering no matter what happiness,
sacrifice no matter what grace.

ETERNAL

Life is sacred from the first moment
and before.
Whether we know it or not,
life is sacred
until the last moment
and after.

GARDEN

Life happens in your mind.
Make it beautiful.
Plant what you love most.
Wander there in solitude
refreshing yourself,
opening to beauty and joy.
There is only time for this.
Tend your garden tenderly
and it will blossom brightly
for the world.

CAN OF WORMS

Lift out one worm,
then another
and another
and so on
until all you have left
is an empty can
and recycle it.

GONE

Like flowers
gliding in the breeze,
opening,
dropping our petals,
we are gone
before we know
we are God.

GREAT SOUL

Like Ganga's crystal-clear sounds
rushing down

snow-covered peaks —
Johann Sebastian Bach
is pure God.

VISITOR

Look!
Up in the night sky
a beautiful Cloud Woman
dances, splashing celestial radiance
at my door!

NEXT LIFE

Maybe I will carry on in my next life
as a poet — taking notes,
humming melodies, spilling out feelings,
entertaining a few, encouraging some,
angering others, confusing many,
causing some to sob uncontrollably,
others to heal spontaneously
and the lucky to laugh.

CAUSES

Maybe you think you are determined
by your genes or your karma—
or that childhood experiences
or social class are more important.

Maybe you believe it's the food you eat.
Or factors like magnetic waves, ghosts or planets.
Maybe you sense how others' actions,
words and thoughts affect you.

Or are convinced that it's all
in the effort you make.
Or it's all in God's hands.
Well, She has sent a poet to tell you:

It is all of the above
and below—and beyond!

PRAYER

May the birds never stop flying.
May the fish never stop swimming.
May the animals never stop roaming.
May the trees never stop breathing.
May the flowers never stop blooming.
May the people never stop loving the Earth.

WELCOMING

May we be clear as the flowing brook,
humble as the crumbling earth,
joyful as radiant laughter,
welcoming as the tree
to every passing thing.

WOMANLY QUALITIES

Men can be good as women
if they want to be
and cultivate their womanly qualities.

Learning to give love, love will be received
and there will be no need to purchase,
prey, steal, rape or kill for it.

Just try to be more like women —
modest, responsible, caring and friendly.
And all of Creation will rejoice.

STAKED

Men not only conquered the Earth
and women's bodies, they invaded their minds
and language itself, staking every natural thing
with ugly labels.

What did the singing Women call the world
before they were silenced?
Before the flowers clamped shut
With their piercing cries?

NOISE

Mind is nothing but chitter-chatter —
chitter chatter, chitter chatter —
nothing but chitter-chatter —
nothing.

LIGHT

Monet was creativity incarnate.
He brushed divine Light onto canvas.
Assuming a human body, he left his dazzling prints —
each stroke a resplendent wave, radiating infinitely.

GREED

More and
more and
more and
more and
more and
more and
more and
more and
more and
more and
more and
more and
more and
more and
more and
more and
more and
more and
more and
more and....

ONE DAY

Mother dwells in every cell
of our body and our world.
Her infinite genius and beauty
permeate all things.

If only we realized this —
and one day we will.

INVOCATION

Mother Earth, it is not you
who need to be invoked —
for you are always here.
But we, your human children
who today must be invoked —
who have abandoned you,
forgotten to call upon you,
neglected to care for you,
failed to serve you
and disregarded your needs.

Help us now to awaken
and remember our obligations to you
and all Earth's beings.
Let your spirit fill us with love,
appreciation, joy and an overwhelming desire
to serve you in all that we do.

May we think, speak and act
as one family of one Mother,
who gives life to all
and when it is time, takes it away.

Guide us, Great Mother,
in every decision we make,
every habit we develop,
every action we undertake.
May we never forget you again,
beloved Mother Earth,
beautiful and bountiful source
and resting place and wonder.

LIGHT

Mother, how can I climb this mountain?
It is too steep! — You must carry me.
I lay my body on your lap
and weep on your heart.
My tears become a pool of light
where I melt sighing *Mother*,
floating effortlessly
one with You.

OFFERING

Mother, I lay my little ego
bruised and ugly, at your feet —

this dark sharp gravelly rock
I made myself that has
no charm whatsoever.

How I love the smooth golden,
rose and white crystal stones
that You made,
polished by your storms
and sliding glaciers over millennia.

I lay my rock such as it is
at your eternal feet,
hoping that by your grace —
some miracle of Love —
it will one day be perfect like You.

SO BIG

Mother, my mind is so small
and You are so big!
To You, I surrender
everything.

VESSEL

My first sentence was: "May I have
a drink of water, please?"
Ever since, You have been trying to fill
my glass and flow unimpeded through me.
Praise, oh Divine Mother, for this one
pure moment of service to You.

HER WOMB

Mother's Womb
of birth and growth,
return and rebirth,
is open to all —
good, bad,
pure and selfish —
a healing realm
of love and light,
enjoyment and transformation.

TEST

Mother, this lethal illness
is the hardest test

You have ever asked me to take.

You must have a fairly high opinion of me
if You think there is even
the slightest chance I can pass.

Now that You have my full attention,
show me how to endure suffering
and overcome even death.

Will there be more tests to come
or will I graduate—effortlessly
liberated—and simply know.

JANINE

Mother thought this:
Janine should walk across this landscape—
and there I was.
A free woman—*but more loving, more luminous—*
stripped of limits and misguided habits.
*Let her discover Me—*She thought—
and I did.

CURRENT

Mother!
To say her name
turns on the Lamp.
Mother, Mother!
turns it up brighter.
Mother, Mother, Mother!
And speechless we melt together
flooding the earth,
a broad stream coursing to the Ocean.

BLOSSOMS

Mother, whisper
that some day my longing
will melt these walls
and they will fall away like velvet curtains
bursting with sweet blossoms
everywhere!

DESCENT

Moving into the fertile dark
I feel the tug of gold,
russet and black.
Running my subtle hands
through the timeless sands,
I begin my descent
to the bottom of the mystery —
eager, anxious, burning —
no idea what I will encounter.
Take me, oh my Mother,
to your omniscient heart,
the source of all Creation.

FAITH

My faith is growing
in the dark.
Joy cannot wait.
When never happens,
where never stays.
Now is here
and all we have.
Happiness cannot wait any longer.
Light hides in the dark.

LUCKY STAR

My mother used to say,
"Don't worry, she was born
under a lucky Star."

How did it feel to be pawned off
on some faraway star?
Not good.

But today I know she was right.
Thank you, oh Star,
for your constant saving light

that has always shown me
the way no matter
how dark.

POISONS

For decades, my ovary
was perfectly happy
and stayed precisely where it belonged.
But what can an aged ovary do
in a world where poisons

keep appearing on the earth,
in the water, the air, food,
and even in our blood.

Poisons that will last longer
than human history!
Finally drove my ovary crazy.
Large amorphous cells running amok
my body —like the birds that no longer know
where to fly and the bees, that cannot find their hives.
And there is really only one question:
What drove the men to relentlessly
invent all these poisons?
Were they demons in disguise?

PRAISE AND THANKS

My soul found itself in Emily,
Cummings, the Upanishads, Kabir.
Praise and thanks, dear friends,
for revealing Truth and Beauty's blissful realm.

THE OCEAN

Nameless, your knowledge
fills encyclopedias beyond counting,
volumes of time and space ever-flowing,
the infinite ocean that inundates all Creation.

HYMN

Never was I alone when writing poetry.
My heart flowed through words —
first thick and red, then thinner,
clearer, more transparent and pure.
Where did it all go?

I hope it quenched the thirst of those
keen for the truth, nurturing,
fueling our incessant search
and eventual discovery.

Yes, It is here — all around and in us —
flowing as one supreme Hymn.

THE SUPREME SELF

No matter what the mind says,
That gaze gazes
through us.

METAMORPHOSIS

No need to read!
Just listen and you will hear
how a soul became a poem
fluttering on the wind—
each word her breath,
each sentence her heart,
each stanza her soul.

ONE

Nothing is separate.
Everything is one consciousness.
Nothing is separate.
Remember.

MISTAKES

No word can express
the extent of a woman's boredom
with man's brutality.
After all he has done,
he would still be bearable
if he could just keep his mouth closed.
Credibility he lost a long time ago.
But he would still be lovable
if he could humbly admit his mistakes
and join in our caring for Life.

REMEMBERING

Obviously everything is one.
What else could it be?
Who needs philosophies
and scriptures
when the words we need
to hear are tumbling
from the trees
and dripping
from the stars.

—And anyway, in our depths
we know them already.

WHEN I REINCARNATE AS A MAN

Of course, I won't remember
my life as a woman.
It will be a new world,
stripped to the bone by patriarchy, probably.
What will my parents teach me
of my duties to the world?
How will I respond
to my big-boned kingly body?
Will I dimly recall what it means
to be a woman?
What will I do when I can only use
half of my brain at a time?
How will I use my crude strong hands?
Will I be able to feel humility,
surrendering my pride
for the good of all?

THANK YOU

Oh Daffodil! Daphne!
Raindrops!
Growth now visible.
Happy Moment!
Thank You!
Kisses!

THE ROSE

Oh my favorite Flower—
painted by the Great Master,
distilled by the supreme Perfumer—
one day I will drown in your fathomless depths,
releasing my divine scent into yours.

GARDENER

Oh Gardener, weed my wild mind.
Pull out my negative habits by their roots.
Plant in me the seeds of Truth.
Water me with your pristine Love.
Make my shoots grow.
Open my buds with your brilliant gaze
and free my divinity.

WE LIVE

Oh Goddess, Surgeon,
the surgery goes on
and still you will not let me go!
I know You love me but this hurts—

did you forget the anesthesia?

Are you doing this open-heart on purpose?
I know You love Creation,
want us conscious, awake,
aware that we live! All-seeing!
Humbled to grandeur, resurrected to Love.

Then keep on scraping,
cleansing, stitching.
I crave to be well and whole again,
radiant with your healing Touch,
a light in your infinite World.

JOURNEY

Oh Lady,
I have already been
to Sahara and Himalaya
and I know that You
are not done
with me
yet.

GODDESS OF LOVE

Oh Mother, You martyr yourself with Love
without ceasing or rest —
your body given over totally to Love,
commanded endlessly to love,
crushed on the grinding wheel of Love,
reconstituted in the blazing flames of Love,
restored in the cooling waters of Love —
only to take on more burdens
in the holy name of Love.

The more miserable humanity becomes —
the sicker from ignorance —
the more You love.
Your arms reach out to the horizons,
rise up to the heavens
and fall down prostrate with Love.
You are all Love — consumed with Love —
tolerant of nothing but Love.
Even the cross must melt in your Love.

How You love your game of Love —
your only nourishment,
your only peace, your only bliss.
You flow and overflow with Love
overwhelming Love itself!
Oh Great One, You are the soul,
the nature, the eternal truth of Love.

Unspeakable! Ineffable! Goddess!
At your feet we crumble.

HER EYES

Oh, to gaze in that face!
The eyes are Roses of infinity.
I press my face into her endless beauty—
unnamable color, ineffable scent—
and enter.

MANY FLOWERS

On a warm summer evening
the virgin Mary appeared.
She came to show me her flowers—
Mary Lilies and Mary Annes,
Blushing Mary, fragrant Rosemary,
Mary's Purity, Mary's Modesty, Mary's Mettle.
Mary's Bitter Sorrow.
Mary's milk drops, Mary's Prayer,
Mary's Bedstraw, Mary's Shawl,
Mary's Candlestick, Mary's sword,
Mary's Pincushion, Mary's Thorns,

Mary's Leaf, Mary's Berry and Mary's wild roses.
And so many more! Mary Jasmine,
Mary Bells, Mary's star, Little Marys,
Sweet Marys, Virgin Mary May,
Mary's Mint, Mary's Nosegay,
Mary's Pink and Mary's Gold,
Mary's Glory and her Crown.
Mary Love and choirs of Ave Maria!

PATRIARCHY

One day, without a qualm,
I divorced Patriarchy
and ever since I pay little attention
to its chosen gods: money, power,
machinery, danger, violence, lust and death.

Many have tried to change it,
but it has stubbornly refused to change.
Like cancer, it only wants to keep spreading,
destroying everything in its path.
Now only Mother Nature can change it.

HAPPINESS

One kind deed a day
keeps the sorrow away.
Ratiocination is often best avoided.
When we stop thinking, reality returns —
zooming to the present, we are here.
Humility is the foundation of real power.
Confidence plus humility is the trick!

DISASTER PREVENTION

Metastatic Technology
is one of the deadliest cancers
known to humankind.
Left untreated, it can spread everywhere
blocking our antibodies, our natural immunity:
Our moral discrimination.

But there is a preventative vaccine
that has existed since time immemorial:
A Good Example given in a series
when children are young and impressionable.
Please share this life-saving knowledge
wherever you go.

THE WAY

One step
into the Infinite
at a time....

NECTAR OF IMMORTALITY

Only pure Mother
can heal — it is the only balm
that works.

Come droplets of Love
from my Mother —
essence that fills me with bliss.

Divine tincture,
pure medicine,
the only tonic that heals.

THRESHOLD

Only through your Heart
can I step . . . over —

AURORA

On the first night, Aurora sat
on the edge of my bed.
On the second, She bent
and kissed my cheek.
On the third, She entered
and all night the Sun kept rising.
On the fourth, She came late
and bathed me in pure light.

Then the counting stopped
and all the hours became
perpetual Day.

FLOWERS

Overnight they arrive —
daffodils, plum blossoms,
songbirds everywhere!
Mother Nature,
on whom we entirely depend,
may we blossom too.

CARRIED

People ask me, "How is your work going?"
And I reply "What work?"
"Are you producing?" they ask.
"Being produced," I answer —
"She is so prolific!"

Don't they understand?
I am floating down the river
on my way to the Sea.
I do my best to navigate
but mostly, I am just carried.

TO ENDURANCE

Perhaps you are everything,
Endurance, for you last.
Your strength is Life Force itself,
Goddess in a human body,
capable of surviving anything
and continuing to be Life.
Oh, you are sweet!

CREATION

Poetry goes beyond telling
to creating experience,
a moment of life,
like an avalanche heaving down
from a dazzling peak.

POETRY

Poetry is communication—
communion—oneness expressed,
inspiring the opening
of mind to the vast spaces
where anything can happen
and miracles are mundane.

Poetry is the spilling of my heart
to you when I am gone.
Gone where?
No place to go but here
even when we are there.

Poetry is a gift from the One
who conceives and births
just for the ineffable joy of it—
who is pure Existence.

Poetry is nothing more
than Consciousness —
the beauty expressed in all things.

ENCOUNTER

Pure electricity without time or space —
that's what meeting Her was like —
the nameless endless Source
in the small body of a dark
holy girl of the jungle
empowered with pure Mother Light.

I fell in her lap and She engulfed me,
invading, irradiating, transporting me
to ineffable bliss.

MAKING OF A POET

Radiant souls in an invisible realm
quietly conversed:
"Since she loves language,
why don't we keep showering her

with inspiring words —enough to keep her
writing poems for the rest of her life."

THOU

Resplendence art Thou,
incandescence —
Light in every pulsing cell.
Radiance art Thou,
gold of the soul.

RELAX

Rosebud, loosen
your tight outer petals
and let the dew drops roll in.
Relax, spread your petals
and drink in the sunbeams.
Hanging loose, let the old petals fall.
Surrender your soul naked to Love.

THE RULER

Ruled by the ego, people are afraid.
Too scared to see straight,
too sated to act, too jaded to play,
too selfish to love, too greedy to be happy.

Ruled by the soul, people are kind.
Courageously they act, innocently they play,
unselfishly they love and serve
and gratefully they smile.

OATH

See all the sick coming and going
with no hair — that's what Patriarchy has given us.
Are we tired of it yet?
Because it got tired of us a long time ago.
And there is another way.
I swear it on all the bibles ever written
and those too pure to ever be spoken.
I swear it in the name of Love
and on Love Itself.
I swear!

BUTTERFLY

Seize the moment —
you will never see it again.
Do not dream it will wait for you.
Tomorrow — when you go to meet it,
it will not be there.
Seize the moment now
or kiss it goodbye — the shimmering
blue butterfly trilling its wings
on the succulent flower
is taking flight.

NIGHT RIDER

Serpent uncoiling
and mounting on fire!
Flame Self
darting in the mind
of Mother Divine,
charging on her tiger,
shooting ten thousand goddesses
in all directions to slay
the demons and save the Earth.

SHAKTI

Shakti carries us on her wild rampages
and every moment is unending.
Her infinite energy lights the cosmos,
even what hides in the numinous dark.
Her divine smile flash-floods
the world with bliss.

THE SAINT

Sitting on the front steps
to protect the path of the ants —
every life was sacred to her.

She often greeted guests
at Oxford dinners with the question:
"Do you believe in God?"

Letters from striving artists she encouraged —
doing her part to keep not God alive,
but the humans snoring in the dark.

— To Iris Murdoch

GRANDEUR

Sometimes I feel nostalgic
for the old days when I was a stone
and it feels so good to greet my kin —
my sole desire to hold the weight
of a smooth round rock.

Other times I feel my leaves
shimmering gleefully in the dusky breeze.
And not surprisingly sometimes
I prowl the cliffs in the moonlight
and I howl.

Today I have this human body.
At first reluctant, I resisted,
but eventually I found the light
streaming in and out of me.
Now to our human grandeur, I bow.

STREAMS

Some words bear no resemblance
to words — are more like rivers
flowing from God —
streaming from the brilliant Sun —
silencing us.

ALL POWERFUL LIFE

Sorry, runaway Cells,
you know how I hate to kill,
but you are incompatible with my life.
Nature's strongest potion —
white gold and yew fungi —
floods my veins.

Go peacefully and humbly to your death.
Your energy must flow where it is needed.
All powerful Life, that knows and creates,
heals and destroys, is on its way.

GOING HOME

Spirituality
is out real connection
to Reality,
the magnetic force
that draws us inevitably
to our real location
in Being.
That guides us
home.

STRESSING OUT

Stress all the way out into the ether — and let it go!
Place the stress on the big syllable — and let it roll!
Keep the stress where it belongs — but not for long.
No need to blow up — inhale and exhale it.
Maintain your rhythm, your sweet and your sour.
Pinnacle or cynical, let it sprout!
Eat, excrete, devour, refuse it.
Finally, choose it — and it will work out.

— For Sophia Schwartz-Cutler

THE INSTRUMENT

I am stretched on the loom,
woven in Tantra —
though I do not even know what Tantra is.
The gods are having their way with me
and I dissolve in bliss —
feeble instrument in the hands of the great Virtuoso.
"Play me!" cries every atom and every gap between.
"Play me — and never stop playing!"

THE BRIDGE

Suffering envelops you
until all the pain fuses into the bridge
you must walk over
to survive.

SURRENDER

Surrender to the tide
that washes over you, carrying you
where you do not know.

Surrender unresisting
to not knowing, to accepting
even the pain sloshing in your heart.

Surrender to grief and rage,
to failure and falling,
to losing and dissolving, and dying, yes dying.

Surrender even to the dark you never wanted to know.
To the forces that pull and sweep and crush you
until you have no control.

Surrender to the tide
that takes you —
and let it all go.

ROOTS

Tapping into the ultimate Power
is the effort that brings
grace rushing in a thousand-fold,
infusing us with the universal remedy:
the boundless Love, the infinite Consciousness,
the supreme Presence in us.

YOUR MESSAGE

Teacher, in our depths
we can hear your message.
It is already inscribed on our walls
and shining in our cells.
Our blood is pulsing with it.
Above us, the Moon and stars hum with it.
It enlivens the limp and gathers the lost.
Every day it gives us our joy.

Only the Sleepwalkers are deaf—
they keep on walking and never wake up.

PATIENCE

Testosterones rule who do not honor
the sanctity of Creation —
addicts poisoned against life and its care.
In a Nano-second, She could wipe them all out
but her fierce Love hesitates.
Patience, She sighs
again and again
and again.

THANKS

Thanks, oh Mother,
for this time You have given me
to utter the single sentence
of my life.

And please forgive me
for all my mistakes.

UGLINESS

Thank you, Ugliness,
for showing me Beauty
with such mind-shattering clarity.

PARADOX

The Absolute says there is a deadline
but will not say when.
If we fail to meet it, we can take the course again.

The Absolute is detached and advises us to be patient,
and enjoy every moment
with the wondrous innocence of a child.

When will I understand the Mind of the Absolute?
Anything goes, it seems,
until it doesn't.

REFUGE

The animals have come out of the forest.
They are sitting in the bar.
They growl.
It is the age of Unconsciousness.
There is no escape or refuge

except in the love
we can draw from our hearts
in the knowledge that they are all me
and we are all one.

THE BATHER

The bather steps reverently into the River,
scoops the Goddess flowing
into her hands,
splashes Her joyfully onto her head
and submerges into her bliss.

BODY AND SOUL

The body is flowing downward
to rejoin the earth.
How the body must long
for clay and ash and worms.

Once the body reaches the earth,
the soul will be free to rise and drift away —
the soul that no one knows or sees.
Except for the Seers who say it is a vapor,
it is Light, it is God's very essence.

Where will it go, the soul, without its cloak,
its root, its reason?
Surely it came for some purpose,
some assignment or duty — some role in Creation.
Will it be happy to be free?
Will it enjoy the next stop on the journey
or be lonely and sorry?

And those who do not believe
what they cannot see with their soft brief eyes,
will kneel on the gravestone and cry,
trembling with fear as their bodies
keep flowing downward —
back down into the earth.

SEEKER

The clown who keeps running
after Infinity.

GUIDE ME

The Cosmic Ocean has no height or depth.
You are that boundless space.
In the immeasurable mystery, hold my hand tight —
Mother, keep guiding me.

BLESSINGS

The creek that was dry, now is full.
The heart that was parched, now is flowing.
The flowers that were buds, now are blooming.
Life rises and falls
and the blessings keep coming!

FLICKER

The day Culture died I felt so sad.
And every day since, I feel sadder—
as if I lost my best friends
who now exist only in memory.

To whom shall I tell my stories
when there is no one to recognize
either the names or events?
And language itself lies dying.

To whom shall I give these precious books,
music instruments and paintings?
Will they be dumped in the landfill
along with the plastic?

The day culture died
was the day billions of hearts
came thudding to a halt,
replaced by machines.

It is pointless to expect a machine
to desire a true education
or want to understand
life's deepest truths.

But we must not allow
our own hearts to stop beating!
It takes such extreme measures

to keep our hopes burning.

Maybe if we can prevent other hearts from breaking,
we will not notice our own pain
and be able to keep on smiling
and laughing.

We have forgotten each of us is a lantern
with a flame inside — no matter how sooty.
If we stay focused on the spark, I think we can make it
through this dark passage.

OM

The flower of the mind is spreading open.
Words float by on the great screen
and condense into one divine syllable.

LIFE FORCE

The force of Life rises fiercely from the Earth.
Assaults cannot stop it.
It rises again and again and again.
Revival is its very nature.

TRUE

The foundation is unwavering Love—
values built up from the beginning,
refined until each human being
can stand true.

ONE MAN, SIX HUNDRED WOMEN

The front door was bolted!
She ran to the bathroom, locked it
and screamed out the window.
But no one came.
Breaking the lock, he dragged her across the floor
punching her in the temples.
"I don't need you," he yelled.
"I have already had six hundred women!"
Afterward he asked,
"Did you like it?"

EACH DAY

The future is waiting with open arms —
you think.
The mind is a toy —
eventually you put it away.
Heaven waits —
let each day show you
its Love.

THE CYCLE

The glass fills up
until you reach
God.

The glass empties out
until you reach
God.

INSIDE THE STONE

The Goddess keeps on carving
and refining her unwieldy stone.
One day its pure soul will be released.
Then where will it go?

BUTTERFLY

The Great Butterfly
landed on Earth
for a few dazzling decades
and the effects will ripple forever and ever.

THE FIRE

The great collection of books and art
gone up in flames in an hour
like the bright sands
of a mandala brushed away
by the gods.

Carved bronzes melted
into pools of holiness.
Story, song, scripture and history
distilled to perfect knowledge,
wisdom and beauty.

The collective awareness of artist,
thinker, poet and seer
returned to pure Consciousness —
scattered in the very air
we breathe.

> —to Ramanand Tiwari, Kathmandhu
> and Pilgrims Bookhouse

LADDER OF LOVE

The ladder of Love goes so far
and fades in a luminous mist.
Midway up, I cannot see
what happens beyond.

I only see you, Mother,
and there are no words
for your magnificence — in awe I stare
at your grandeur and mystery.

I, a tiny toddler blundering
rung by rung.
Oh my beloved Mother,
do not let me fall!

MELODY OF THE UNIVERSE

Then let these books crumble
and flow with the mud
down to the sea.

Let them become part
of the ever-moving
earth and water.

Let their words return
to the essence
they came from.

Syllable by syllable,
let them merge
in the melody of the universe.

Let them go
where they want to go
and are needed.

SOUNDS OF ETERNITY

The nonexistent poet
composes a nonexistent poem.
Too subtle to be heard,
it sounds and fades.
No pen or paper needed
for words inscribed
in the Silence.

ANNIHILATION

The North Pole shifts westward
as Earth's core sloshes turbulently —
relentlessly agitated by the greedy inhuman beings.
Forgive them, Mother —

for they know not what they do
and worse, do not want to know.
They deny the evil they have wrought and blame
others.
They are lazy and cruel — forgive us all!

May Creation's radiance awaken man
from his headstrong stupor —
his stubborn commitment to be as selfish as possible
no matter how bitter the end.

Light beings hover, showing the Way.
But their wreckage is everywhere.
If only they would leave Mother alone!
she could heal the massive wounds they ceaselessly
inflict upon her.

Dangers clamor louder and louder!
The devils, afraid of losing their power,
posture up and dig in their heels, salivating for war —
the final destruction of everything not them.

They have been fantasizing violence for so long

that hatred pervades and perverts every cell.
Their minds are flooded with scenarios of
annihilation —
demolished forests, gang-raped women, rivers of
poison, nuclear winters,
shredded atmosphere and dead oceans.

Orgiastically they draw their guns
to shoot the birds, the women and schoolfuls of
children, shoppers, concert-goers, and sanctuaries
where the seekers gather.
They even set fires to raze the forests and towns.

Violence is the privilege they claim,
domination their birth-right, they say.
Ignorance is their core principle;
ugliness their way.

Frenetically they race their Egos,
terrified that having used up
everything on Earth,
they, too, will soon be extinct.

OWL

The owl moved from the redwood tree.
There was too much commotion —
tearing down ivy, sawing off branches —
and then, a fence!

She moved to the tree next door
where the humans, older,
had finished their "improvements".
And tonight when the moon is full and soft,
she coos like a dove — throaty,
chuckling, lost amid the branches.

Oh how her voice takes over the night.
Night after night she calls her hooty song
from the black black world —
glowing white as the moon —
her eyes all over us.

HUMAN HISTORY

The past died
and history vanished.
You might say, isn't that good
since life only occurs
in the present?

But the present died too.
People turned into machines.
And need I speak of the future?

NOW

"The past is a cancelled check," says Amma.
It is gone, so let it go.
How many hours, years, centuries
have we wasted holding on?

This is the weight of history
that bogs us down—the boulder
of regret, resentment,
bondage and failure.

Let us rise to the present moment
fresh and new,
see the amazing flower
and pluck the fruit hanging ripe now.

THE PATRIARCH

The patriarch holds tyranny
in his right iron fist
and bloody revolution in his left.
War, rape, over-population are his favorites.
Destruction is the rotten fruit
of his doomed rule.

MAGIC

The poet is the magician
who puts what cannot be put into words
into words.

REALITY

The present is not only the best
but the only place
to live.

FREEDOM

The purpose of freedom
is to be free
to give yourself
away.

THE MEN'S MARATHON

The race
to the goal
of total annihilation.

THE REAL BIBLE

The real bible is endless —
volumes beyond counting.
Only a madwoman attempts to read it
and melts in space.

The real bible holds every existent truth,
every illuminating idea
that can ever be articulated
and not one unnecessary syllable.

It can only be read by an immortal,
since mortals expire long
before finishing it —
which takes all of eternity.

It explains all about life and how to live it,
but its radiance is so powerful
that only a Goddess can touch it
and not be zapped to zero.

So beautiful and transporting is it
that reading is indeed unthinkable —
each line so inspiring that one follows its instructions
and manifests its revelations immediately.

Written on pure Consciousness, where each page
is so chaste that words rarely show themselves,
the real bible must be read directly
from the Author's Mind.

PROBLEM

The real problem with God
is us — the sense of us
that believes it is all
there is.

OPTION

There is a war
going on between mankind and Nature.
Guess who is going to win.

Of course, we could
surrender.

BEYOND

There is beyond
and beyond the beyond
and beyond the beyond beyond—
oh beyond and beyond and forever beyond!

EXPERIENCE

There is no way to tell the truth
with only your tongue.
Only through experience can it be known
and only then, be told.

THE RIVER

The River flushes and cleanses
and makes me pure,
clearing the darkness,
washing the dregs —
all the refuse my soul refuses
carried away!
Now only You are here.
Oh praise!

ESSENCE

The River is flooding — it is boundless.
There is no end to the stream
of poetry — how will I ever
complete my work?

— Oh Poet, be calm!
Pluck out a few sparkling drops
of pure essence
and be happy.

ALL THAT MATTERS

The scribe writes on the flowing water.
The doctor digs into the earth.
The child climbs into the lap of heaven.
Being Yours is all that matters,
all that really is.

MOON AND ME

The song I wrote in the Moon
sang back to me, "I love you."
"I love you too, Moon,
how your soft face watches tenderly,
where a lover's word can always
be secretly inscribed,
how you glow through the night
and peek through the clouds."

"I love you, my poet," continued the Moon,
"how you write me your dreams,
your pains and visions —
pouring your whole heart into my pallor,
filling me with the truth no man sees.
I love your poet soul that weeps
and sings with endless Love
for human possibility."

NEIGHBORS

The stars came jumping down!
(More wanted to come but stayed in their places
They came to shower bright smiles on our faces
and set us swinging.
Dipper and Orion were twinkling.
"Guess what's out there," they whispered.
"You haven't forgotten us, have you?
We never forget you, poor things!
If only we could help more.
We keep shining our lights
but it is you who must take the steps."

MOTHER

The stars come down to sit in your lap
and feel your timeless touch.

Even the wicked fall on their knees
to be lifted and loved by You.

RISING AND FALLING

The Sun rises in the darkness
and the Divine Woman slowly rises out of the ground.
Rolling up she stretches out her arm
and takes one step—and so begins
the Dance all over again.
Standing on one leg, She turns
and out of Herself untwists the entire Universe.
The Sun rises high and brilliant.
Golden days spread in peace.
Life grows in forms unimaginable
as the Sun floats over the cloudy light blue sky.
Then the dusk settles onto the Earth.
Invisibly She dances and the night falls again.
Lowering her body step by step
back down into the Earth,
She curls up and rests
and sleeps.

THE CRIME

The supreme crime of patriarchy
is the destruction of the respect, love and trust
between mother and daughter,
the mother-line,
the heart-line of humanity.

THE SONG

The Violinist asks, "Did you enjoy my music?
I practiced, sacrificed and performed.
Listen and I will play again!"
"Wait," cries the Soul, "that was me!
All I learned from lifetimes poured into your playing.
I am the voice that sings through you."

Then across Creation boundless laughter roared.
"Who wills it all but I who dream this world
and others you know nothing of.
I am violin, soul and song."

THE WHEEL

Over and over the wheel is reinvented —
detour after detour, failure after failure,
heads bloodied again and again on the rocks.
It is humiliating, lonely and frightening to be lost.
Grandmothers weep in the darkness.

THE WORD

The word "God" has become a problem
and many have cast it away.
But how can we ever throw out its meaning?
Fortunately — since everything is God —
there is no end to how we can see,
say, describe, be awed by or deny it.
It erupts perpetually — geyser of truth,
beauty, purpose, joy, mystery and peace.

Only when we are truly human
will we begin to understand
what it means.

DESIRES

This world was designed not for the ego
but for the Soul.
If we try to fulfill all our personal desires
we will be very disappointed.

ONE DROP

This drop,
boiled down from all the drops
of tears,
I lay at your feet,
oh Mother.

AWAKEN, SLEEPERS

This is all a dream—a pastel landscape
that occasionally brightens
to searing joy and pain.
A dream that will only end
when we wake.

THIS LIFE

This life is my offering.
What else could it be?
I watch it burning in the rapturous flames
that eternally crave life.

GRANDEUR

This mere inkling, Mother,
of how great You are
is the most precious thing I own.
To it, may I surrender again and again.
And one day find the courage
to dive all the way into the grandeur.

BEATITUDE

This vale of tears,
this unbelievable opportunity,
this possibility
to know,
to love,
to be.

MADNESS

This world, Mother,
this world boils in agony.
All its thoughts have gone mad.
On fire with madness,

its roots long forgotten,
there is no peace.

Oh Mother, hold the world close —
blow out these raging fires
burning us up!

EVERY DAY

Time flows eternally.
Sunday, Monday, Tuesday, Wednesday —
every day is equally precious,
every moment divine.

GRAIL

Time is the crystal grail that holds
the holy drink of knowledge and happiness —
the immortal nectar of Now.

BOWING

Time runs out.
Petals droop, leaves drop.
The poet's words lie prostrate,
longing to be nothing but an endless bow.

HARD ROAD

Today everything is upside down!
It's all about money, machines
and keeping patriarchy afloat.
That's why I got divorced and set out
on the path to Beauty, Truth and Goodness.
It's a hard road to walk these days —
but aren't they all?
And this one is worth it!

DARKER

Today explorers of goodness are rare.
Most people huddle in a dark muddle of sin
and do not even go for a short hike.

Here and there a lamp shines.
It grows darker and darker.
Harder and harder to see all the stars
sparkling in the forever and ever.

AMBROSIA

Today I drank pure Mother —
which cannot be described, only drunk.
Sweeter than the sweetest
and brighter than the brightest —
I drank pure Mother
and melted in her golden heart.

GODDESS REALM

Today I went to a gathering with a Goddess
in a realm bubbling sweet chants and pure light.
She held me in her arms, crying "Daughter!"
and now I never want to leave —
this love, this beauty, this peace.

In the realm of the Goddess there is no illness —
only sublime perfection.

Your heart is mine and the cosmos
throbs with Love—and Love, I promise you,
is more real than anything.

I have gone to Devi Loka
where everything is so beautiful.
I did not expect such divine Light!
Gone to Devi Loka where the Goddesses
are shimmering!

TEARS OF AN OLD PSYCHIATRIST

Today, most people call
for addictive prescriptions or financial support.
This was not my original intention.
My aim for the patients perpetually arriving on my
doorstep
was always more knowledge and less suffering.
Often I wondered why so many settle for so little.
I longed to go all the way to the Sun—*Know Thyself.*

"Patient," from the Greek root,
means "sufferer"—and no one crosses
a psychiatrist's threshold on a lark.
But this much suffering should not be!
Humans have become expert at wrong living.

Shallow, debauched, society drags relentlessly onward
toward ignorance and destruction.

How can a mere psychiatrist elbow her way in?
Replaced by rapid-fire script writers —
wage slaves of the rampant Corporation —
old psychiatrists hunch on the sidelines
trying to block Psyche's frantically flickering flame
from the unbridled gales of disaster
wailing around every corner.

IMPERMANENCE

Today my hair
fell into my hands.
"Impermanence,"
sighed the passing winds.
I went into the garden
and buried it in the mushy
winter leaves for the songbirds
to wind in their nests
come Spring.

GRACE

To me, She often came in invisible words.
To others naked green in the woods.
To others in the cacophony of the multitude.
To each, She comes in her own perfect way.

RELIGIO

To reconnect and remember
our place in Creation
and beyond —
our ultimate bond.
Let's clear the old religions
of their muddle,
liberate the great Souls
from their cages
and experience
what is eternally here.

PERFECT CHANCE

Truth is all-pervasive.
Imagining it separate and single,
I attach like a leech
while the whole universe flows on —
unaware that every moment
is a perfect chance to experience
supreme Consciousness itself.

RADIANT

Uncover the heart
of your heart — the golden point
that radiates light everywhere.

JEANNE OF THE CONGO

Unlike Joan of Arc,
she was not burned at the stake —
but tied to a tree and raped
by gangs for weeks.
After her first surgery,
the men resumed their raping,

forcing her to give birth ringed by guns.
Fortunately, the infant died or no doubt
they would have raped and killed it too.

Now young Jeanne, small and dark,
struggles to the stage
and speaks out with the loud voice,
the laser focus and the fury of pure virtue.
Her mouth is my mouth roaring from Bukavuto,
Sonoma, every city on Earth.
Are you tired yet of your domineering
pornographing predatory lusting
after the power of demons?

Are you satisfied yet — ugly, cruel,
stupid, useless, vicious, hateful —
not even human?
You stole the sacred body
of a human being
and desecrate it every time
you dishonor
a woman.

OM

Volumes of the divine Syllable
cascade from the Eternal

plunging into torrents
and streaming to the Ocean,
making all One.

GOLDEN AGE

Was I one of your hunters, Mother,
amidst the buzzing bees —
so very long ago
when I first stepped
onto this sweet path?
What were we hunting
when paradise was drenched in golden light,
euphoric birdsong
and falling ripe persimmons?
I must have offered You
my heart's ruby-red rose.
For ever since, as far as I can remember,
I have craved to merge
in your perfect Love.

THREAD

We are hanging by a thread
of Love
spiraling
through Eternity.

HERE

We are sparks of Consciousness
creating many worlds.
We are buds of cosmic bliss.
The Absolute is not elsewhere —
it is here — always unfolding.
A pure silence full
of vast music.

JOY

We cannot wait any longer
to experience joy.
We must do it even while
we are suffering!

RECOVERY

We have heard the teachings over and over —
kindness, compassion, devotion —
now we to need to live them.
Sand away negativities and egotism,
open our pores to what really is
and feel It once again.

LIVES

We have probably had hundreds and thousands
of lives — more than words can ever say,
than there are words —
more and more.
We have lived in the stars
and rocks, butterflies and ants,
galloping four-legged over savannahs,
wandering upright chanting,
bending under the sun crying,
swishing long skirts and flying on the wind.
Oh you gods, forever beside me,
with this tongue, this wing, these feet,
this leaf — this light —
I praise Thee
every one.

THE SAME

We may not be able to see
the same things
but we are
the same Consciousness.

THE HARP

What artisan made that exquisite instrument
shipped from Boston past Cape Horn
to the City of the Queen
to appear one Christmas morning
to a thirteen-year-old longing for a harp?
She first saw one in a gilded frame
hanging over her grandmother's sofa—
tall, golden, strummed
by a woman in a long pink dress
sitting by a woman in blue singing.
How she wanted to be pure as that music
rippling dazzling through the air.
Drawing the heavy wing onto her small shoulder,
she dropped her fingers into the strings
and plucked out a rainbow.
So began her journey to become so pure
she would one day simplify heaven
and resonate with the stars.

LIGHT

What does the Light feel
when it wakes up in the morning
and falls asleep at night —
pours all over the Earth
or holds a small bird in its beam?

FOR SALE

What does no marketing,
has no market
and is not for sale?

HOMO SAPIENS

Whatever I said that was bitter and burning
was not burning enough
to describe what we, the Earth
and our children, have been put through.

There can be no words
for the horror of this holocaust.

And still they go on—madmen stripping,
plundering, gang-raping their own Mother.

In a second, She can brush all the termites away.
And when the shack collapses,
floods sweep everything out
and the Sun dries all the rot to dust?

When there is nothing left to eat
and no one left to remember?
When Homo Sapiens dies from all the poisons
he cavalierly heaped on the Earth?

When beauty, sweetness, caring and birth are gone
and there is only starvation
under a ravaging Sun whose golden veil
he tore from her face.

When there is no life left to kill—
not one man, woman, bird,
cow, fish or bug—
will he, even then, be done?

TESTOSTERONE SOUP

What if a whole box of salt
was poured into your soup.

Would you want
to eat it?
Would you
like it?
Would you eat it
anyway?

DIVINE PLAY

What is She practicing —
the great One —
aspiring toward? —
what does She mean to be? —
the great enigma, the mystery,
the virgin spring,
the changeless, ever-changing
eternal Source.

THE PRIZE

What is the point of a poet
who does not even reach
for the impossible prize blazing
beyond speech?

MIRACLES

What is this talk of miracles?
This is all miracles!
Look.

BALANCE

When humanity tilts the scale of life to one side,
what offering can bring the scales back into balance?
When humanity heartlessly takes everything —
what can we give but our own hearts?
If we place all our Love on the empty plate,
will it balance the mountain of Selfishness
on the other side?

HARMONY

When I reincarnate,
maybe I will find these poems
and they will speak to me.
Maybe I will set my favorites to melody
or illustrate them with mandalas of earth and oil.

Maybe Sappho, Mirabai, Emily and I will be best
friends
and sing in a chorus of heavenly harmony.
Or maybe I will forget it all —
and be free to wander chanting
one simple hymn of joy.

A GOOD MAN

When my father read the newspaper,
I doubt he thought of it as made
of pure consciousness — but he acted as if he did,
holding it in his left hand, carefully folding each page
back with a gentle pat.

Today people rarely read the newspaper,
or focus their minds, or know tenderness.
But in those days when my father
read the newspaper,
I felt their mutual respect.

VANISHING ACT

When our identification
with our small mind
and our mortal body dissipates
and we identify with all that exists,
all our worries, questions and discomforts
will vanish, promise the enlightened,
as we evaporate into the totality.

THE SINGERS

When the singers close their mouths,
slipping through the hall of no return
into the dazzling light of the Choirs,
may we remember forever
their exhilarating songs
in our hearts.

HABITS

When this Janine routine is over
and the physical apparatus
that makes it possible disintegrates,

will my soul rise in a vapor
transferring the record of everything
I thought, said and did?

And after a pleasant vacation on another plane,
will it start playing back my habits,
nagging me to repeat them,
until I have to struggle all over again
to tear myself free?
Oh you gods, spare me!

RIPE

When the time is right
and I am ripe,
You will harvest me.
May I grow sweet
yet retain my tang
when You swallow me.
Like a gong resonating
in the silence.
A pebble tossed into the lake
rippling to the shore.

REVERSING COURSE

When we walk away from the truth
while eloquently talking about it,
may we hear our blather,
turn around and obey.

I

Which
I?

FINAL SOLUTION

Why is a new poison —
worse than the last —
Patriarchy's typical idea
of a solution?

THE RIVER

Why struggle?
The River will take you
where it wants.
Just let go
and let it carry you.
It will show you the way.

OH MUSE

Won't you ever leave me alone?
Won't you ever fall asleep?
Will you never tell me your real name?
Hiding behind this word or that
like a nun in her habit;
changing identities
like a wandering flower child;
unpredictable as a glistening chameleon;
shifty as a kaleidoscope;
sublime as a saint —
will you never tell me
who you really are?

BLOODY WORLD

Women are tired, getting more and more tired.
We are exhausted by the ways men bleed
and keep on bleeding us,
spilling blood all over the world.

There is no place without their bloodshed.
Men's bloody world, bloody ways.
We are done, we are moving on.
Come if you want to change.

THE FORCE

Women, blast through the barriers
of domination
with the force of Life
that you are!

RIGHT

Women do most of the planet's work
and men do what they wish —
this is "male privilege."

Women birth and nurture men
who exploit and abuse them with impunity—
this is "male domination."
Men claim ownership of the world
and women scramble for safety—
this is the grim right men inherit and kill for.

MEMORANDA

Words are reminders—*beautiful, wretched!*
Not the very thing itself,
but reminders
of what we experience.
Sadness, happiness—little words
that remind us.

THE MYSTERY

Words cannot hold the River.
Words cannot understand Creation.
Words can only pray to serve
the Mystery.

TONGUE TIED

Words, disturbed, molested and trafficked—
words made of vibration, thought and experience—
each of you a precious bud that can open.
You speak to the birds, the mountains, the Sun.
In thousands of languages—a vast symphony—
you chatter, sing, protest, yearn and pray.

But most of you are tongue-tied—
unspoken—heard only in the realm
where everything gathers in silence.

WORDS

Words have roots
that reach back to the beginning
and stretch to the very end—

draw life from the mind that harbors them
and never stop craving
the Light.

SINS OF THE FATHERS

Worse than their extreme greed
is their mad contempt for Life
at the bottom of their never-ending campaign
to conquer Nature — their demonic will
to dominate Life to extinction.

CREATION

Write it on my body,
inscribe your Light in me.
Burn your beam in every cell.
Set me ablaze with your search-light.
Wash me in rainbows and churning waves.
Pound me fresh and new.

Mother, I am your daughter.
Poet, I am your poem.
Goddess, I am your creation —
the sun of your splendor,
your infinite Light.

A BREATH

Writing a poem is like saying,
Wind, take me—carry me
with the dust to the invisible.

Let my words be brushed away
like the colorful sands
of a monk's mandala.

I am ink on paper in a library
that will, like all the rest, fall down.
I am merely a gesture of love.

A breath exhaled for no reason.
A simple sign of life.
An instant in the created world.

A desire. A decision.
One more passing proof
of the incomprehensibility of the Mystery.

Take me, Wind, whenever,
wherever you will.

HOLY

Written in us are holy words
that bring no pain and cause no rage
and silently melt the heart,
that do not wound
but flow in all-suffusing Love
and cannot be expunged.

TEACHER

You are my doorway to the truth,
my anchor in the truth,
my experience of the truth,
my precious Teacher.

INCARNATION

You are so
God!

THE LOTUS

You are the living Lotus whose colors
cannot be named.
Words dissolve in the Source.
In the heart Eternity waxes and wanes
in endless shades of light and dark.
Like drunken insects, the Sun and Moon
dote on your ravishing petals.
And we are mere toddlers
splashing, reveling in the mud.

MYSTERY

You came to me,
lying in limbo
in a scanning machine,
Cosmic Boa,
with the unmistakable
dark-haired head of the Goddess,
coiling and cocooning—all around
the bulky contraption You wound,
weaving your amazing knot,
swaddling me in eternity.
Unknowable to me are your ways,
Great Mother, but thanks,
oh thanks!

OH ETERNAL

You have all the time in the world
because all of time
belongs to You
who are yourself immortal.

The bell in the graveyard
stands still
when You appear
in your unimagined Glory.

The sullen world breaks forth
in praise, rejoicing!
Oh Eternal, You never leave,
for your Love is undying.

ARCHER

You have pierced my heart!
With every breath I take
the Arrow cuts deeper.
There is no question
of taking it out —
I am staked.

TO YOU

You who are the line of mothers,
the lineage of teachers,
the succession of goddesses
and their Source,
the reality of pure Love,
the supreme Consciousness
that moves in all things,
Creation and Creator,
To You, I bow
and bow.

AFTERWORDS

Writing is a mirror that reflects the writer's thoughts, feelings, memories and visions. It reflects who and what we are. It is an expression, an action, a response and also feedback. For the reader it may be entertainment, recognition, revelation, displeasure, or nothing. For the explorer on a journey it is evidence of worlds visited — a record. When it spontaneously overflows like the song of a bird it is one of the purest, most direct forms of human communication. A poet may call, recall, envision, prophesy, lament, exult, realize, harmonize, mock, loathe, rage, pray, implore, incite, pontificate, illuminate, weep and adore. And the reader or listener, the other eye and ear, either closes the book and stops reading or takes it all in. The sacred literature of civilizations has been written as poetry.

In my youth I observed the world and wrote about what I saw as I felt it. I observed the inner world and allowed my unconscious mind to present itself. Outer and inner worlds mingled freely. I indulged in imagination, painted pictures with words, told stories and dreams, dredged the unconscious, gathered imagery from anywhere — I let it stream like Joyce. Each collection seemed to show what needed to happen next — like a step on a path that was leading...I really didn't know where. I wrote on an old Royal typewriter, "I am tapping my way in the dark." I carried e e cummings with me wherever I went. I remember thinking, if only I could write one beautiful poem, it would be enough. I started writing short prose poems like my friend Phyllis Koestenbaum, integrating experience, fantasy and dream, in an increasingly luscious, upsurging language influenced by the oceanic novels of Iris Murdoch.

At first I wanted to learn to convey feeling, then I realized thoughts could be included too. I wrote longer and more expansive forms—an extended address, "Dear Body," an overpowering supplication to "Our Lady," a first-person biography of the "Passion of Georgia O'Keeffe." The narrative urge eventually expanded into a series of short stories, *Journeys with Justine*, followed by a volume of essays, *Goddesses, Goddesses,* then another in 2015, *My Millennium: Culture, Spirituality, and the Divine Feminine.*

Gradually it dawned that I was responsible for what I wrote, for the personal, social and spiritual impact of my words—no matter how small my audience. Though mostly I could not know its effect, my writing had consequences—like anyone's offspring, raised then released into the world beyond our control. The young German poet and philosopher Goethe had learned this painfully at twenty-five when he published *Sorrows of Young Werther* in 1774 and unleashed a wave of suicides across the country. Increasingly I understood that it was my duty—as well as my joy—to share what I was learning and experiencing on a higher not only a personal level—not that this could be silenced anyway—it was bursting out all over.

In the recent decades of this Dark Age in which materialism and intellect predominate over spirit, heart and human values, a number of American authors have proclaimed that they write in order to find out what they think. There are many ways to find out what we think as well as feel: There is thought itself—thinking it through; there is contemplation, meditation, psychotherapy, art, play therapy, dream-work, automatic and left-handed writing, journaling, and good old conversation. As modern Western stream-of-consciousness writers and psychoanalysts, along with ancient Eastern seers and meditators pre-dating written history, have graphically demonstrated, thoughts are incessantly, countlessly and limitlessly happening in the human mind. Finding out what we think might be the worst nightmare of all—an unending archeological dig through the world's greatest garbage dump.

Isn't Art, though sometimes therapeutic for the artist, really something of an entirely different order? Shouldn't Art, in every genre, take us beyond our personal desires to a universal realm of illumination available to everyone—a realm "where beauty is truth, truth beauty," as the English poet Keats wrote. Isn't the role of the artist more of a midwife enabling that birth, a messenger leading us onward toward a larger, truer and more beautiful truth? Art, I feel, is something that ventures via imagination beyond the limitations of the reasoning mind into the infinite mind of the Cosmos. I believe that

> A poet does not write to find out what she thinks
> but to open her heart to the great Song
> and find out what it thinks.

Words arise from the unconscious, the conscious and also the super-conscious mind. Those of the higher mind are the most powerful, important and truthful words of all. When the mind becomes clear, we can hear the voice of truth, and see the Light that is always truly trying to guide us.

It was my literary guru Iris Murdoch who first pointed me in this direction when she asked, over lunch in the Berkeley hills, if I had ever had any visions. I, like most people, had and I heard in her words an instruction to write about them. But it was my spiritual guru Amma who later made me realize how much humanity needs to be lifted up and inspired—and that whatever work we do, we should do it as a spiritual action that benefits others, not only ourselves. This awakening intensified my admiration for the tender and compassionate poetry of Mary Oliver, the magnificent soulful work of Maya Angelou, and of all who create from the eternal Soul. No matter how virulently allergic our *tout est permis* culture is to concepts of responsibility, morality and duty, let us hasten all the more urgently and bravely to administer the only healing allergen that can save our anxious humanity and plagued planet from succumbing altogether to the blindly selfish, appallingly careless, anti-social and life-defying—in a word, wicked—ways of patriarchy. If the ways we are now living are upside down—once called "wrong"—isn't that exactly why we should "vision the way we should be living"—and isn't that "the responsibility of poets"? So three poets—Janine, Judy Grahn, Kris Brandenburger—wove it together one afternoon under a wise oak tree.

My own writing has always been and increasingly is an expression of my personal search for the truth. My spiritual journey and my journey as a writer cannot be separated. My mother sang songs and read fairytales to her daughters at bedtime—from her I received the gift of a close friendship with literature. Elementary school teachers, all women, nurtured my schoolmates and me with books, poetry, plays, singing, dancing, painting, history, arithmetic—and play! At night I jotted down thoughts—not really thoughts, a phrase, some conclusion or essence gleaned from the thoughts passing through my mind—on little pieces of paper, storing them in the drawer by my bed before I fell asleep. We were formally introduced to American literature in junior high, and in high school a creative writing class was offered—from which I recall composing a poem about the connection between the generations—which is the definition of human culture.

In the exuberant sixties, temporarily derailed from my intention to become a psychiatrist, in part by a notoriously misogynist Stanford advisor, I went on to major in French where I felt more secure—thanks to my outstanding high school French teacher Mlle. Lida Clementi, graduating "with distinction." I then pursued graduate study in German at the University of California in Berkeley, so I could read, above all, Rilke. In coffee houses I immersed myself in poetry hot off the press—Rexroth, Duncan, Griffin, Ginsburg, et al—and began studying masters of Western and Eastern psychology, philosophy and spirituality. I craved knowledge about almost anything, but above all about the ultimate nature of reality, what we are, and why we are really here.

During my humanistic Presbyterian childhood, spiritual practices included prayer, hymns, scriptural readings, good deeds and community responsibility—it was a good grounding. With curiosity I explored the Abrahamic tradition in my teens, while experiencing the subtle vibrations of the Indian Yogi Sri Yogananda residing in nearby north Los Angeles. In our backyard I tried and failed to assemble the neighborhood kids into yogic pyramids. I began to learn how to meditate, chant mantra, and do simple yoga in my twenties. My thirties were primarily consumed by medical, then psychiatric training, and trying to keep up with my demanding Muse. Whatever else was going on, I was always writing. My first book of poems, a collection of portraits, *Of Your Seed*, came out from Berkeley's Oyez Press with a National Endowment for the Arts' grant during my Residency. Other poetry collections soon followed. In those days I thought a lot about creativity, as well as mental illness. My spiritual practices remained sketchy, my convictions hazy and confused.

Over the early decades of my life I explored various religious pathways—Christian, Indigenous, Jewish, Hindu, Buddhist, Sufi, New Age, Goddess and so forth. In midlife my search intensified, but it was not until a personally shattering event suddenly swept me—one sad but beautiful spring evening—on a magic carpet into the lap of a teacher of the highest order—a living saint who walked her talk in every moment wherever she went in the world, a soul at the highest level of spiritual attainment, a human embodiment of pure Consciousness, Love and Compassion—that I finally found my path. Sri Mata Amritanandamayi, known in the West as "Amma, the hugging saint"—simply called Mother by most—had begun her annual tours of the world in 1987, and soon after what would become a phenomenal global volunteer network embracing state-of-the art medical care and education for all, collaborative international scientific research, traditional arts and medicine, sanitation, clean water, sustainable villages, organic farming and widespread tree planting, youth and women's empowerment projects, natural disaster relief, and food, clothing, housing and pensions for the very poor. At 48—"midway on the journey of life" (*Divine Comedy*)—I had met a spiritual master of such magnitude that my search came to a halt.

After a period of incredulous observation, blown-away awe and streaming tears at the discovery that pure unconditional Love actually does exist (and unknown to me was already healing old wounds), I eventually became aware that it was time for me to get down to the serious work of revising my imperfect personality and really start learning. Many can speak the truth, but how many can live it? Amma's rare example inspired me to start gathering collections of her

powerful, bold and uplifting teachings for our chaotic time —
first in *Messages from Amma* ("A Health & Spirituality Best
Spiritual Book 2004"), then in a small pocketbook of 108
quotations, *Garland of Love,* and finally in *Love Is My
Religion,* a 3-volume collection of thousands of quotations.
Collections of my own writing expressing my journey since
meeting Amma include *Ardor: Poems of Life, Mystic Bliss:
Poems* (bilingual in German), *My Millennium: Culture,
Spirituality and the Divine Feminine,* and *Consciousness.*

As with any writer, my own writing — its vision,
texture, focus, tone and style — has spontaneously unfolded
over time, like a flower passing through its various phases to
arrive today at what seems to me a simple, distilled, deeply
felt, sometimes didactic, often ecstatic form. "Very spare and
intense, addressing just the essence of things," a close friend,
Aija Kanbergs, recently wrote. But I was always compelled
to brief and concise expressions. Always a mystic, I knew
early on that everything is one, everything matters, time is
limited and death near. And that knowing fueled my ever
burning desire to know more and go deeper. Now so many
poems remain among hillocks of unpublished work stored in
boxes, unattended because life is only a moment.

May all of us love, enjoy and benefit from the
precious experiences that Life gives us, may we share our
good with others, and leave something helpful behind, no
matter how small it is.

Women and language cannot be separated. Women are the
womb not only of human life but also of human language.
From birth onward children learn language above all from
their mothers. The ability to hear matures in the first month
of life as a baby hears the sound of its Mother's voice talking,
whispering, cooing and singing into its tiny ear. Over the

next years the child internalizes the sounds, words, meaning and structure of language, first learning to speak, then read and write its mother tongue. In women the cortical language centers of the brain are larger, more active, more highly developed and more abstract in function than in men. According to consistent studies, women excel in communication, demonstrating superior language skills and a greater capacity to listen. It is therefore unsurprising that the first recorded poet and novelist were women — Enheduanna of third millennium BCE Sumer and Lady Murasaki of medieval Japan. Even when constrained by the cruelest of shackles by thousands of years of patriarchy, women have excelled as language teachers, singers, storytellers, readers, writers, poets and philosophers.

I was born a feminist — without thinking about it, I simply loved nearly all things feminine and happily immersed myself in them. This was easy, since I grew up in a family of females, my mother, two sisters, and even my father who was fairly female too. As a girl, I gravitated toward books written by women: the *Little House* books by twentieth century American novelist Laura Ingalls Wilder, introduced to me by one of our motherly school-teachers at 42nd Street School in Los Angeles; *Heidi* by the nineteenth century Swiss sage Johanna Spyri, which I received from my grandmother Flora on my ninth birthday and re-read with awe at age seventy-four; *Little Women* by the super-prolific nineteenth century transcendentalist, feminist and abolitionist novelist Louisa May Alcott, given to me by my parents; the *Nancy Drew Mystery Stories* of Mildred Benson, gifted by a neighborhood mother whose grown daughter had read them all. By fourteen I was soaking up my mother's illustrated edition of Charlotte Bronte's *Jane Eyre,* and taking the cross-town bus to Hollywood's literary temple, Pickwick

Books, discovering all the Bronte sisters. And finally, from my parents I received for my high school graduation the newly published, three-volume Harvard Edition of the complete *Poems of Emily Dickinson*—one of the supreme poets of all time.

In my thirties, after graduating from New York University School of Medicine, while traveling in the Yucatan, I would discover on *Isla Mujeres*, the Island of Women, the work of Anglo-Irish novelist and philosopher Iris Murdoch—as passionate a feminist as all those above—who would become my beloved literary guru and influence my increasingly exuberant writing style, from a collection of prose poems, *Shapes of Self*, through the prose to follow. Of American women authors still alive during my adulthood, I was most strongly drawn to the beautiful, moving novelistic masterpieces of Leslie Silko, the multi-faceted, life-embracing work of Goddess Maya Angelou, as well as the humbling, compassionate Nature poetry of Mary Oliver. Laura, Johanna, Louisa, Mildred, Charlotte, Emily, Iris, Leslie, Maya, Mary—a blood-thrilling and unstoppable stream of female creative power, continuously blessing people all around the world—women daring to write about life from their own experience in a world made by and for men. Is that one of their great-great-granddaughters twittering today from Canada—named Rupi Kaur?

Feminism became conscious for me when the Second Wave struck the shores of the sixties and seventies and never stopped rolling in for us Second Wavers. We are still and will always be waving to women everywhere our impassioned durable support for women to become stronger and more effective, and save the world with their God-given gifts of love, empathy, creativity, fertility, beauty and intelligence. Women alone have wombs that produce life, breasts and hearts that nurture life, ever-ready whole brains that function on both sides simultaneously. Women are the mothers of this world, the mothers of every single human being who has ever been born anywhere at any time in human history. We all owe Women a debt that can neither be estimated nor repaid. At least we should offer women our vast gratitude, respect and compassion, as well as our willingness to act with strength and commitment on behalf of all women today and in the future. This is every woman's and every man's basic duty.

What tool is more powerful than the words we speak and those we write? Words are so powerful that we must use them with utmost respect, discrimination and care. A word can be used as a weapon of love or hate, good or evil. I believe that when we think of the words that arouse goodness in us and inspire us to positive, creative and transformational action, that is when we are most deeply stimulated to heal, grow and act. I think of the countless women authors through written history, going back to the first known poet, the High Priestess Enheduanna of 23rd c. BCE Sumer, onward to the first creator of a novel, Lady Murasaki of 12th century Japan, to the female singers, poets, philosophers and visionaries of medieval Europe and Asia, such as the legendary Benedictine Abbess Hildegard von Bingen, the enclosed mystic poet Julian of Norwich, the wandering singers Lalla and Mira, the first Bengali poet Chandravati who authored India's epic *Ramayana*, the Mexican Baroque genius Juana Inés de la Cruz—through the numerous remarkable women of the Renaissance, Enlightenment and Romantic Era, to the countless women now writing on every continent. Ever since there has been speech, there have been women speaking; ever since there has been writing, there have been women writing. And so I cannot help wondering who made the alphabets used in the first written words and sentences if not those whom Mother Nature most generously endowed with the capacity for language.

All the female genius hidden behind narrow walls, suffocating shrouds and tombstones ever since the insanity of male domination began, shows us that there is an insuppressible and indestructible Life Force that inhabits all creation and especially women. To our Mothers let us bow, to their unknowable struggles, their silent suffering, their unbelievable endurance, their burning courage and relentless trail-blazing, the adamantine light they have always shone in the darkest of times, their indescribable inner strength and boundless wisdom. We can see them all sparkling on the rising tide of the Third Wave of the Women's Movement now flooding us with Women's Marches—*Me Too, Time's Up, Black Lives Matter, March for our Lives*—and drenching the news, law-courts and politics of every nation, every male-female relationship and interaction, as mounting numbers of women choose to stand up and claim their birthright, their primal heritage and their eternal duty.

And high time!!!

Almost all of my own work comes from direct inspiration. So I do not really know why I translated Else Lasker-Schueler and Francis Jammes. I was in Berlin in 1966 at the time of the publication of a centenary edition of Else's collected works. I remember seeing the red book featured on the table in the middle of the room. I knew her work only vaguely from my German studies at the University of California. I bought it and took it back to my room in an old 19th century building in one of the neighborhoods that had not been bombed out. Shortly after opening it, I started to translate—over the years translating many more poems than I ever published in *Star in My Forehead.* In the end, I chose the poems that had the most meaning for me at the time. I always felt I was meant to do this task. Lasker-Schueler was relatively unknown in America, and I empathized with her as a solitary bohemian visionary woman poet, driven from her homeland by mad and violent men—forever into the realm of the Word.

My connection with Francis Jammes, strangely born the same winter as Else, was similarly guided. Discovering a bilingual selection of some of his poems in a Berkeley bookstore, I was immediately drawn to their candid childlike innocence, and wanted to read and translate more of them. I think I felt it would be a way of being with the poems more deeply and intimately. Eventually in Paris, where I have spent considerable time, loving French culture as I do, I found a small fine edition of the complete Jammes in a well-known bookstore on the Left Bank. As I was thumbing through it, the compelling thought presented itself that I should translate a fuller collection of his work—and I was hooked. I had to suspend other work to complete *Under the Azure*, and as with other literary undertakings could have spent the rest of my life realizing and perfecting just that one book. Jammes, little known in the secular USA, was a deeply spiritual poet like myself who found himself increasingly out of tune with his time.

With both poets my approach was to immerse myself in the work as if I were merging with the poet him or herself, and proceed word by word, trying to translate as precisely as possible both the surface and the deeper meaning, the broader associations and the organic root resonances. Translation is an enjoyable and even mystical process for me because of my passionate love of language. In the Indo-European languages, the Sanskrit word for "the Word" is Vak. Vak is the Mother of Speech first described in writing in the *Rigveda*, a collection of hymns and verses downloaded by ancient seers, men and women of pre-historical northwest India. Transcribed in Sanskrit around 1500 BCE, it was eventually included in the *Vedas*, India's great book of Sacred Knowledge. Vak is another name or aspect of Saraswati, the Supreme Goddess of Wisdom and Art who holds a lute-like instrument on her lap and rides a beautiful white Swan over the pulsating ocean of Creation.

Beloved of seers, sages and poets, Saraswati embodies the powers of vision, knowledge and creativity which allow us to perceive and comprehend the nature of existence and express it in coherent verbal form. She offers the amazing riches of language, the power of naming, the capacity to think and communicate, and thereby grants friendship and community. Too subtle to be grasped by human intelligence, She can nevertheless make us understand. She gives meaning to sound, not only the sounds of human speech, but all the sounds of Nature. According to the ancient Vedas, in the beginning there was sound, and the sound was OM, the sound of creation. As John the disciple of Christ put it later, "In the beginning was the Word, and the Word was with God, and the Word was God." More recently, scientists have discovered that the essence of creation is Energy in the form of sound waves that hum like OM. The whole world, they too say, is humming!

Today, sixty-five hundred languages are spoken around the world. English is spoken by a fifth of the human population—one and a half billion people. Approximately three hundred sixty million people speak it as their mother tongue. English is an international language, rich, diverse and complex. Mixed with its Germanic roots are many other languages, including Celtic, Latin, Greek, Old Norse, Italian and especially French; and many words from Chinese, Hindi,

Urdu, Japanese, Dutch, Spanish, as well as other tongues, have expanded its inclusive vocabulary. Because of geographic and historical proximity, the German and French languages offer unique opportunities for the translator to bring over into English not only meanings, but also sounds, rhythms, syntax, grammatical structure, texture and flavor. In the end, however, English has its own distinctive personality, sensitivity, tone and flow, and any translation into English must be shaped and adapted to allow its natural rhythm and music to be heard. We have to accept that a translation will always remain a translation and will never be the original—which must be spoken in the mother tongue of its author. Writing and reading are experiential. Just as the poet tries by various means to articulate their initial inspiration, the translator tries to convey, as skillfully, movingly and persuasively as possible, the experience of a poem created in a language not their own.

Works of art are created out of nothing, anything and everything. We could even say that poetry itself is nothing more than translation — "carrying over" into words something ultimately intangible and beyond words that comes from an unknown language, spoken in an unknown realm. And that is its very magic. Language is one of the greatest of our human mysteries.

In the human brain the creative state operates on a *theta* wavelength even slower and more amplified, both higher and deeper than typical alpha waves of the relaxed mind of a meditator, or anyone experiencing a moment of harmony. The normal, wakeful, logical, problem-solving mind operates on tense, short, rapid beta waves. Dreams occur at various frequencies—alpha, beta, desynchronous—during the second "rapid-eye-movement" stage of sleep. But as we enter sleep, we enter the theta state, which is the deepest place the conscious human mind can go before experiencing the long, slow, leisurely delta waves of deep sleep—when we do not experience personal consciousness at all (though amazingly, we can still talk.) The theta state is where creativity takes place. It is where creative people in all fields live or at least vacation frequently. I can feel myself slipping into it wherever that might be—at home, communing with Nature, enjoying a musical concert, beholding an inspiring painting in a museum. A voice of a different kind, recognizable as a lifelong presence, whispers some words that are not heard with the senses, but in some way known. These, if given full attention—which I, as a poet, dutifully and eagerly offer— often roll on into a poem. This is normally called Inspiration, or the Muse, or Intuition, or Heart. And it is crucial for every artist to hold this state as long as possible. Where does it come from? Anywhere, everywhere, within, without. It comes on its own, according to its own will, and the only way to receive its unpredictable gifts is to obey it like an adoring, utterly willing slave. Because it knows better than the rational mind ever can; that is, knows things the rational mind never can. Whether seen, heard or felt, this is what the artist tries to capture.

We can say that the creative process is a kind of mindfulness or meditation if we understand that after relaxing our bodies, letting go of our thoughts and surrendering to the intuitive mind, we must also be prepared to put what is revealed to us into concrete form. Otherwise, the gift of Inspiration is wasted and there is no artwork, scientific formula or invention to share with humanity. A truly creative person is a conduit and a servant—a seer, an actor and a benefactor. A poet can utilize all kinds of forms— for example, a lullaby, a prayer, a love song, a lamentation, exhortation, commemoration, hymn, allegory, aphorism, witticism or quip. But without the urge to share it, a poem or a story would never come into being. There would be no literary art at all. For art is actually Love and never meant for oneself alone.

Art is the deepest kind of personal sharing. It is a gift from the artist to the world. It links the individual to society, and vice versa. As the twentieth century American poet Charles Olsen put it, "Poetry is the personal made public" and in another context, "A poem is energy transferred from where the poet got it, by way of the poem itself to, all the way over to the reader." Anyone who ignores their inspirations, wastes their talents and is excessively self-indulgent in self-expression — though they might occasionally move, entertain and inform us — should not be confused with a serious artist who dedicates their life to their art and gives to it all he or she possesses. A real artist lives mostly in the present and incessantly strives to improve their artistry, hoping someday to reach the supreme goal of perfection. Supreme artists, like Monet, Menuhin, Angelou, Dickinson and Shakespeare, set the highest standards for all privileged to experience their absolute devotion. Such beings are closer to living gods and goddesses than mortals and have the power to carry their devotees to extraordinary heights of awareness, joy and even bliss.

The hard-to-describe intensity of the creative process is well illustrated in Paul Haesaerts' 1950 film documentary "Visit to Picasso," in which the perpetually inspired painter paints on glass while a camera rolls behind it. The overflowing artist cannot stop. Brush strokes of colorful oils dart in all directions in a rapid-fire, boundless outburst of fecundity, incessantly changing and unfolding, adding then subtracting layer upon layer up to the final moment when for no obvious reason, the painter stops — or is it rather that the roll of film runs out and the camera clicks off? Creativity is really nothing more than the ability to tap into the incessant stream of creation in which all of us — as part of Nature — play the role of both observer and creator. Once you know how to do that, once you can let yourself go there, you will experience the deliciously irresistible, timeless taste of pleasure so familiar to artists. As Mata Amritanandamayi once said, "Art is one of the best ways to discover the pure and blissful consciousness of the true Self."

In my own life, I try to maintain a meditative practice of awareness and compassion at all times. The spectrum of my practices has included sitting and walking meditation, prayer, mantra, yoga, singing, dancing, spiritual reading, contemplation, watching the mind, social action, festivals, charity, helpfulness, thankfulness and laughter. All are good ways to achieve higher consciousness and can be adapted to the limitations of age, illness and disability. Failure is always part of the process. My work, both as psychiatrist and writer, has probably been my principal mode of practice, and spirituality pervades all my activities increasingly. I try to apply love, compassion and understanding to my work and use everything as a vehicle for growth and transformation, as a form of meditation and prayer. Yes, I believe that writing should be mindful — that we should, ideally, be mindful of every word we write or say or even think. My greatest desire as a writer is to serve as an instrument of the supreme Creator.

Poetry, indeed all art, arises from life as a natural expression of Life itself. One of my apparently most affecting poems, "Dear Body," came to me while I was swimming. I had to climb out of the pool while it streamed on. Water was dripping all over the paper as I wrote, even while climbing into my car to drive home to my typewriter, where the poem carried on to completion. Many poems have come to me while driving and I try to scribble them down on paper. They usually come when I am at the ocean, and I have often had to chant them continuously until I reached pen and paper. In recent years they frequently come when I am meditating, and I have to decide whether to interrupt my meditation to jot them down or not. Nowadays I tend to let them flow by — like sand mandalas brushed away by a monk's hand. Some may have been good — maybe the best ones of all. In a way I experience everything as poetry now, so I am not so attached to a single poem. I just watch the shimmering fish surfacing and diving back into the Sea. Who could ever write it all down — even the great geniuses offer only a brief glimpse. A madwoman, ecstatic and determined, once tried to catch them all. The ones she never caught, are they still there? Watch and you may see them waiting for you.

What attracts me to poetry? What a stunning question! I haven't the faintest idea but am pretty sure that in my last life I must have begged mightily for a life full of Art — for that I have certainly had. My home, my education and my very nature provided me with extraordinary exposure to all the arts — and for that, the depth of my gratitude cannot be measured. From among them, the one I chose for myself was poetry. I was mesmerized by poetry from the start, so perhaps I should say that Poetry chose me — and I could not resist. Was it already inherent within me? Have I been a poet before? — no doubt a poetry lover. Is everyone potentially a poet? I was always in love with words, certain words, those that awakened me, made me feel, stirred spreading rings of thought, hooked and drew me quivering into the potent magic and mystery of Language itself—that unseen bridge between human beings and the Unknowable.

Most of my writing has been poetry—that is what comes naturally—and when I write prose I am aware that it is the prose of a poet, not of a prose writer *per se*. For me, every exhaled syllable and every inhaled pause counts, has meaning and presence, even personality. The sound, tone, beat, melody, resonance, dissonance, harmony, nuance, allusion, association, implication of every word—its history, its meaning, its feeling and vitality—matters. And there are an awful lot of syllables, words and pauses in a prose work to keep track of, whether in a short story, an essay, or that all-inclusive object, a novel. Even as a prose reader I read slowly and deeply as if reading a poem, and if the writing is not doing enough, is not deep enough, I rarely finish a book, perusing it at best. Objective prose writing is a necessity for many practical purposes in life, but I personally prefer to flow with the Stream in whatever I am doing, especially speaking. Language is so voluptuous and gorgeous, so full, rich, musical and universal, so pleasing, fun, playful and unlimited in its possibilities. Every word in the dictionary is at our disposal, and if the right word does not exist, a poet is free to create it, or dip into another language or lingo. "The difference between poetry and prose," as my friend Jude Cameron puts it, "is like the difference between singing and talking.

In general, prose writing requires more words and works best for concrete and practical matters. In certain ways it allows us to say more. It seems to give us automatic permission to say almost anything, if we will only follow the basic rules—grammar, syntax, spelling and logic. But for poetry there are no rules. Poets can make up their own words, their own spellings, their own grammar, their own word order, their own forms, even their own facts. In the context of a poem, two and two can be five without being untrue. Poetry aspires to explore the fathomless depths and untouchable heights of mind and world, to reach the invisible realms of intuition and nuance, and melt language into the mystery of meaning itself. However sensuous, it craves distillation. Poetry seeks to condense phenomena to essence. However effusive, it wants to say the most with the least. Poetry is always teetering on the brink of silence. It wants to go where simplicity and brevity are more powerful than anything, And to do that, it is willing to sacrifice its most precious possession: words. Poetry, that chats with the stars, the worms and the gods, is literature's most intimate and universal form. It will reveal its innermost riddles to anyone. Poetry is breath, one inhalation and exhalation after the next, until finally there is only silence. The arc of my own *oeuvre* has seemed to move from expansion to contraction—from a growing interest in the inner life of people toward an expanding narrative urge that in later years slowly condensed into an ever more distilled and simplified poetry— described recently by a friend as "very spare and intense, addressing just the essence of things."

Sadly, we cannot realistically expect an uncultured, undereducated and hyperactive society like ours to appreciate poetry. Its news, nuance and ambition are far too subtle. Few Americans possess either the culture, education or concentration required to really experience any art. Our numbed populace demands melodrama, noise, vulgarity, obscenity, blasphemy, hostility and violence to awaken them from their deep apathy and attract their fleeting attention. Needless to say, this has been a very painful development for all who dedicate their lives to language arts, indeed all who are aware of the profound importance of preserving living cultures and healthy societies. Many servants of the future are working industriously, both solo and in groups, to prevent the total loss of our artistic heritages.

But the destruction continues. When I was growing up, there was a genuine appreciation of poetry in American culture. For cultured people worldwide, life without poetry was unthinkable. For some time now, education has given short shrift to literature, ethics and timeless wisdom, while placing money and livelihood center stage. In only a few decades, esteemed colleges have devolved into business schools, and the concept of a general cultural education has almost entirely disappeared. I was grief-stricken in the eighties when poetry was somehow taken over by academia and declined into something I no longer recognized as poetry — something intellectual, shallow, prosaic and soulless. But that was only an early sign of a culture already in decay — a culture plunging deeper and deeper into an abyss of meaningless materialism, rampant narcissism, run-amok addiction, continuous warfare, societal chaos, and unlimited immorality. In the twenty-first century, we have witnessed an epidemic of greed, waste, exhibitionism, exploitation, untruthfulness, animosity and violence that have reached grotesque levels and infected the entire world. Will the prevailing atmosphere get even uglier, many wonder. Will we and Earth's other creatures even survive?

And yet thankfully, in response to the stunning and ever-mushrooming offense of this era, I and others increasingly observe indications of a moral reawakening — explicit references to the importance of cultural, spiritual and human values. In the domain of literature I have seen the reappearance of real poetry. In this extremely challenging darkness, in which all that lives and breathes is literally at stake, I see a light brighter than ever before emerging from many directions—signs of a rebirth of responsibility, unselfishness, caring and self-sacrifice; signs of hope, courage and faith in a larger happening in which every single one of us plays a necessary role. For we are, without exception, interconnected and inseparable. May we finally shift towards a desperately needed renewal of ethics, morality, connection and compassion in every sphere of life. The responses of many of the young to our situation inspire hope. I notice beauty, wisdom and poetry from the heart, spoken in a language more sensitive to life and sourced in authentic inner experience, which pleases me enormously. And I am grateful and relieved.

For a budding author called to write, the first encounter with a truly great author is a profoundly unforgettable experience. Emily Dickinson was that author for me. The massive awe I felt before her deluging poetic power, I still feel every time I summon the courage to approach one of her poems. The word *poem* seems inadequate for that level of attainment— the purity and truth that a supreme master of words can convey with a mere handful of sounds. We can only bow before such a phenomenon. Drinking the ambrosial syllables, the thirsty reader experiences an expansion of consciousness that only a poet who is also a Seer can bring about—and then, only if the reader is willing to abandon the confines of ordinary thinking to *see* what the Seer reveals.

Another deeply meaningful experience in my life as an author-in-the-making was meeting my literary guru Iris Murdoch in my thirties. Having been introduced to her work through her short shocking novel *A Severed Head* in the midst of a battering hurricane on Isla Mujeres, I felt deeply honored to meet the great writer five years later at the University of California. Iris was a warm, kind, curious and encouraging person, and a passionate feminist. When she said, "You are indeed a poet," I thundered within. "How you can make one *feel*," she wrote in one letter. Iris was a strong role model and a beloved mentor for me as well as many other writers until her death. "Onward, onward with thinking and writing!" she cheered. I described our first encounters in the essay "A Visit from Iris," published eventually in *Goddesses, Goddesses: Essays*, as well as in story form in *Journeys with Justine*.

As a mature author, my most memorable experiences have been the appreciations expressed by readers who have been affected by my work and kept a book close, consuming it voraciously, reading certain poems over and over. Once after a reading, a woman told me that she felt my poetry had healed wounds she didn't even know she had. Such personal and candid responses have given me real joy because poetry always had a similar importance for me. When I was really in need and wanted something more, hungered for beauty and desired a deeper truth, it was Poetry I often turned to. Walking to my bookshelf, I would pull out a volume of poetry and fill myself—for me, it was soul food. If a poem of mine gives someone else even a moment of beauty, I am satisfied. If something I have written nourishes, sustains, encourages, gives hope and light, meaning and value—something the reader really needs to proceed on the journey of life—it is all worth it.

The expression of appreciation completes the circle of love that Art should be and really is. After the pleasure of sharing the poems anthologized in *She Rises like the Sun: Invocations of the Goddess by Contemporary American Women Poets*, it was very nice to receive the Koppelman Award for best-edited feminist work, and it means even more to know that out of print, it continues to be useful in Women's

Studies and Spirituality programs. It is deeply meaningful to me that, thanks to the Navajo Literacy Project, *Walk Now in Beauty: The Legend of Changing Woman*, a short illustrated book based on much study is bringing back one of the Navajo's most beautiful and sacred stories to children whose vital wisdom traditions have undergone horrific devastation.

One of my most satisfying and humbling experiences as an author took place in my psychiatric office. A patient who kept a copy of *Messages from Amma: In the Language of the Heart* on her coffee table, was about to receive a visit from her mother-in-law, a fundamentalist Christian from the Midwest. Debating whether to remove the book and avoid possible offense, she decided to simply be herself and leave it out in full view. As she left for work the next morning after her mother-in-law's arrival, she saw her reach for the book. When she returned in the evening, her husband's mother was sitting with the book still in her hands. "I like this book!" she said. The story made me glow not only because a bridge had been crossed between a mother and daughter, but also because the goal of the book—indeed one of my greatest desires as an author—had been fulfilled. The love in Amma's messages had succeeded in speaking over the gulf of differences in background, culture, age, class and religion that too often separate us.

At some point in later years, I asked myself why I really write books and realized that the real reason is communication, even communion. However triggered, words arise from within us, but writers do not write them down merely for themselves. We write for those who read and receive them. Art, any art, does not and cannot exist without others to enjoy it. It is created either for other people, or as a direct expression to pure Being. Conscientiously, patiently and painstakingly, the artist shapes and reshapes, tunes and fine-tunes, clarifies and amplifies, invigorates and simplifies. Why? To make the work worthy of the inspiration, the glimmer of truth and beauty entrusted to the artist, and of the receiver who wishes and needs to be inspired. Artists works out of a deep desire to connect and communicate seamlessly, leaving no trace of the effort involved. They share their love for the light that illumined a moment. They alter a word or a line, a brush-stroke or a color, a note or a key, to better convey their experience so the audience too can see, feel and understand its meaning and ramifications, connect them to his or her life, resonate with them through analogous experiences, and push open more inner doors. The artist wants to wake people up, stir their inner life and fill it with Light!

The river and source of Inspiration — Consciousness itself — will always flow. It will never run dry. Every time a painter or a poet reviews a work, he or she sees and feels and understands something fresh and new. That is why the French poet Paul Valéry famously said, *Un poème n'est jamais fini, juste abandonné* — "a poem is never finished, simply abandoned." Personally, I cannot resist revising my poems even after they are published. In the early and late collections of Whitman, Moore, Auden and others, who can say which of the various versions is the final poem? Rarely is a word set in stone so that not even a syllable can be budged. Only Supreme Being is that perfect. A perfect work of art, such as the music of J. S. Bach, is pure transmission of Being itself.

In the end — the pause we call death — every poem, everything that is, has to be left behind — either surrendered or taken. Each poem, each story, becomes just one more offering to What Is — one more expression of thanks and praise. Writers and other artists share their momentary experiences with whatever artistry we can. Gaining in craft as we continue to practice, we expand our ability to feel, appreciate and communicate Life, and in so doing become more aware of the Grandeur in which all beings take part.

—from "Conversations with Authors: Janine Canan," *The Zarf Blog*, June 6, 2018

ACKNOWLEDGMENTS

Deep gratitude for the appreciation and encouragement of readers and editors Laura Amazzone, Barbara Brooker, Z Budapest, June Cotner, Carol Fabric, Andrew Harvey, Robert Hawley, Linda Johnsen, Mara Keller, Katherine Lage, Nancy Leatzow, Lynn Lonidier, Paul Mariah, Joan Marler, Karen Mattern, Kimberly Moore, Musawa, Darlene Phillips and others.

Some of these poems were first published in the journals *Amma's Forest Dwellers, Ann Arbor Review, Companions of Light, Matruvani, Mother House of the Goddess, Poetry Nook Magazine, Sonoma Valley Sun, Synchronized Chaos* and *Tower Journal;* the anthologies *Back to Joy: Little Reminders to Help Us Through Tough Times* and *Earth Blessings: Prayers, Poems and Prose Honoring the Earth,* edited by June Cotner, *Light the Flame: 365 Days of Prayer,* edited by Andrew Harvey, and *Diamond Cutters,* edited by Andrew Harvey and Jay Ramsey, *Digging Our Poetic Roots — Poets of Sonoma County,* edited by Katherine Hastings, *She Rises: Why Goddess Feminism, Activism or Spirituality,* edited by Helen Hwang, and *We'Moon Gaia Calendars,* edited by Musawa, et al.

PRAISE for the poetry of JANINE CANAN

"Nothing less than an ongoing dialogue between writer and universe."
—Mary Mackey, author of *The Earthsong Trilogy*

"Inspiration itself dressed as a poet. A crowning achievement!"
—Linda Johnsen, author of *The Living Goddess*

"Gorgeous lyric and prose poetry. Her work reflects her view of the art as 'a calling, a gift, a devotion, a duty and finally a mystery.' Brava!"
—Phyllis Koestenbaum, author of *Criminal Sonnets*

"Such a Soul Poet! This will be a classic."
— Z Budapest, author of *The Goddess in the Office*

"Her finely attuned sense of the inner relation between self and the other makes her unique in the art of verbal portraiture. "
—Gary Gach, author of *Pause, Breathe, Smile*

"The true poet removes the cataract from our clouded eye so we can see the Beauty and the Mystery. Janine Canan is such a poet."
—Anne Baring, author of *The Dream of the Cosmos*

"Her love of language and love of life are poured onto every page for our pleasure and inspiration."
—Mara Keller, author of *Persephone*

"Again Janine has opened her sparkling net filled with quietly luminous words, arranged with effortless perfection, balanced and true—each poem an intimate portal where we emerge renewed."
—Joan Marler, founding editor of the *Journal of Archaeomythology*

"A primer about being. The poems are often simple, declarative sentences that make comprehension of our vast, complex and beautiful life accessible."
—Margreta von Pein, author of "Linguistic Knowledge in Learners of ASL"

"Distinguished poems."
—James Laughlin, publisher of New Directions

"Absolutely excellent."
—David Meltzer, author of *When I Was a Poet*

"Vast in scope and courageous."
—Mary Ann Sullivan, founding editor of *The Tower Journal*

"There is a lot of light in Janine and it streams in and out of her poems. When you read them, you feel better."
—Andrei Codrescu, author of *Messiah*

"Wonderful powerful poems! How she can make one feel."
—Dame Iris Murdoch, author of *The Sea, the Sea.*

"A rich collection of poetic genius. A wonderful opportunity to see the world from the eyes of a prophet."
—Jaylan Salah, *Synchronized Chaos*

"A contemporary mystic whose soulful weaving of words evokes the divine love, passion and devotion of the medieval Mirabai, Lalla, Teresa, and Hildegard."
—Laura Amazzone, author of *Goddess Durga and Sacred Female Power*

"Canan sings, affirms and celebrates the divine feminine, the Goddess in us all."
—Alma Villanueva, author of *Song of the Golden Scorpion*

"Another Emily Dickinson, and as original."
—Lynn Lonidier, author of *The Rhyme of the Aged Mariness*

"There's an energy within that hearkens to *musica universalis*. It is Canan's prowess that she can draw from everything to manifest how Poetry Can Be About Anything."
—Eileen Tabios, *Galatea Resurrects*

"Lyrical, fresh, unadorned, and often surprising. I didn't want the book to end."
—Vicki Noble, author of *Shakti Woman*

"Astonishing poetry, very pure. A book you keep by your side like a bible."
—Barbara Rose Brooker, author of *Love, Sometimes*

"This simplicity, so luminous and radical, is the Mother's last and highest gift to a devotee, the one brave and wild enough to be burnt away in her furnace to become one of her embodied flames of love and sacred passion."
—Andrew Harvey, author of *Savage Grace*

The seed of Poetry planted in me was nurtured by my mother who loved the arts, a good public school education, a great humanistic university education, and meetings with remarkable Western psychoanalysts and Eastern spiritual masters culminating in the supreme living teacher Mata Amritanandamayi, known as Amma.

Janine Canan lives in California in the Valley of the Moon. In 2009 she received "The Sacred Feminine Award" for her work, which now embraces 21 collections of poetry, essays, stories, translations and anthologies. Her most recent books are *Love Is My Religion* by Mata Amritanandamayi; *Mystic Bliss: Poems; My Millennium: Culture: Spirituality & the Divine Feminine*; and *Garland of Love*, sayings by Amma, and *Ardor*.

Canan graduated from Stanford University *with distinction*, New York University School of Medicine and has been a practicing psychiatrist for forty years, and for several decades a follower of the renowned hugging saint and humanitarian, Mata Amritanandamayi. Janine began writing poetry as a child in Los Angeles and her first collection, *Of Your Seed,* was published through a National Endowment for the Arts grant. Her anthology *She Rises like the Sun: Invocations of the Goddess by Contemporary American Women Poets* received the Susan Koppelman Award for best-edited feminist work; and her first gathering of Sri Mata Amritanandamayi's teachings, *Messages from Amma: In the Language of the Heart,* received *Health & Spirituality*'s "Best Spiritual Book 2004".

Today, Janine's retelling of the Navajo legend of Changing Woman, *Walk Now in Beauty*, is read in the Navajo Literacy Project. Her poetry has been translated into Spanish by the Colombian poet Manuel Cortes-Castaneda and into German by translator Peter Geiger. Her papers are held in the University of Iowa's Special Collections. For further information, please visit JanineCanan.com.